"Forget about snappy dialogue, characterization and plot. It's the pitch that gets a script read and a movie deal done. If it were not for Ken Rotcop, most new writers would be out of the loop."

—John Lippman
Wall Street Journal

"Over the last six years, more than 80 projects at Pitchmart™ have been optioned. The art of pitching, it seems, is one part idea, one part delivery, and about ten parts chutzpah. Ken Rotcop coaches his students on how to make prospective producers fall in love."

—Patricia Ward Biederman
Los Angeles Times

"Two-thirds of the earth's surface is covered with water and the other third is covered with people who have fabulous ideas for shows if only a producer would give them an opportunity. Ken Rotcop, an award-winning writer and producer, provides a guiding light to this group."

—Robert Siegel
All Things Considered
National Public Radio

MICHAEL WIESE PRODUCTIONS
www.mwp.com

Since 1981, Michael Wiese Productions has been dedicated to providing novice and seasoned filmmakers with vital information on all aspects of filmmaking and videomaking. We have published more than 50 books, used in over 500 film schools worldwide.

Our authors are successful industry professionals — they believe that the more knowledge and experience they share with others, the more high-quality films will be made. That's why they spend countless hours writing about the hard stuff: budgeting, financing, directing, marketing, and distribution. Many of our authors, including myself, are often invited to conduct filmmaking seminars around the world.

We truly hope that our publications, seminars, and consulting services will empower you to create enduring films that will last for generations to come.

We're here to help. Let us hear from you.

Sincerely,

Michael Wiese
Publisher, Filmmaker

THE
PERFECT
PITCH

How to Sell Yourself and Your Movie Idea to Hollywood

by
Ken Rotcop

as told to
James K. Shea

edited by
Marlane McGarry

Published by Michael Wiese Productions
11288 Ventura Blvd., Suite 821
Studio City, CA 91604
tel. (818) 379-8799
fax (818) 986-3408
mw@mwp.com
www.mwp.com

Cover Design: Art Hotel
Book Layout: Gina Mansfield

Printed by McNaughton & Gunn, Inc., Saline, Michigan
Manufactured in the United States of America

ISBN 0-941188-31-0

Library of Congress Cataloging-in-Publication Data

Rotcop, Ken
    The perfect pitch: how to sell yourself and your movie idea to
    Hollywood/ by Ken Rotcop as told to James K. Shea.
        p. cm.
    ISBN 0-941188-31-0
    1. Motion picture authorship. I. Shea, James K. II. Title.

PN1996.R74 2001
808.2'3--dc21   00-068533
                                                                CIP

TABLE OF CONTENTS

ACKNOWLEDGMENTS

■ ■ ■

I wish to thank all the executives, agents, and managers who have given so generously of their time to support our Professional Writers Workshop, the Pitchmart™, and the making of this book.

I also want to thank Sandy for her tireless work in getting this book down on paper. I want to thank my wife Connie for taking care of the real world and leaving me alone to write. And I want to thank my dear friend Marlane who came to my rescue, as usual.

And finally, I want to thank my good friend Jim Shea for his friendship, encouragement, and creative contributions.

AUTHOR'S NOTE

For the sake of simplicity and clarity, I have followed the colloquial usage of allowing "he" or "they" to stand for either gender, instead of using "he or she" when the pronoun does not refer to a specific individual. This construction does not imply that all producers, for example, are male. In fact, more and more women are joining the executives ranks of the entertainment industry.

INTRODUCTION
Life's a Pitch.

It can be said that all of life is a constant, ongoing sales pitch. You are selling yourself all the time, in any and all business or social meetings. While the main thrust of this book is about pitching screenplays, the principles apply to any form of sales or business presentation, office get-together, or social interaction.

Like it or not, any time you place yourself before another individual or group, you are pitching. This book presents a few clues about how to do that a bit better.

The thoughts and comments of various people have gone into the making of this book. There are numerous contradictions. Just as there are many ways to ask a girl for a date, or your boss for a raise, there are many different ways to impress, persuade, or cajole an executive to read your screenplay.

You must determine which theories best support you and the creation of *your* Perfect Pitch. Remember, the goal of the Perfect Pitch is to get your script *read*. Once they've agreed to read your screenplay, you better hope and pray it's as good as your pitch!

Ken Rotcop is an award-winning writer and the former creative head of four studios. He runs the Rotcop Professional Writers Workshop and created the Pitchmart™ where production executives come to listen to the pitches of Workshop members. In the past few years, a staggering eighty-plus deals of one kind or another have resulted from the Pitchmart. Furthermore, as of this writing, eleven films have been produced due to the Workshop and Pitchmart. You can contact Ken at: pitchmart@juno.com, or fax him at: (818) 346-2916.

Here, presented in his informal style, are his comments on the Art of the Pitch.

I take a course at New York University from Michelle Cousins. It is my first class in screenwriting. Michelle and I become friends, and when the course is over, she tells me about this terrific idea she has.

She spends two years of her life writing to colleges all around the country that have cinema courses. She gets them to send her screenplays based on the particular region of the country in which the college is located. So a student at Louisiana State University wrote a screenplay about the Bayou country. A University of Maine student submitted a script about a family of New England whalers. A story written by someone at UCLA was about the surfing set.

She collects scripts from all over the country, and prepares to put together a television series called *Images of America*. She even thinks about Norman Rockwell as the host.

It is a very exciting premise. I read through some of the scripts and they are quite good. She asks me to go out and pitch it to ABC, where she has already set up a meeting.

So off I go all by myself, twenty-one years old, to ABC in New York City. I go up in this high-rise building, past desks and desks of secretaries, being led into the office of one of the top executives. The room is filled with six or eight other executives all waiting to hear about *Images in America*.

I am plenty nervous, and it is silly of me, but I've brought along about eight of these scripts. They are piled up in my hands. I can hardly hold onto them, they weigh so much. I plop them down on a desk.

Introductions are made around the room. I am just about to start into my pitch, when suddenly, the door of this executive office is flung open and in comes Mel Brooks. Yes, *the* Mel Brooks!

He races through the office, leaps up on the desk of the head executive, and starts to do a tap dance. Everybody is roaring with laughter. Then he jumps down, grabs me by the hands and says, "It was so nice of you to come in." He picks up my eight scripts and practically throws them at me.

I am doing a balancing act to keep them from falling. He proceeds to lead me out of the office, talking all the time. "It was a great idea. I'm so glad you came in. What a wonderful concept. We really will consider it. Please know that the door is always open." He leads me out of the office, past desk after desk of secretaries, talking non-stop.

The entire place is in an uproar, I am totally humiliated, totally embarrassed, and totally out of my league. I don't know what to say. I don't know what to do. I don't even know who the hell he is!

He takes me to the elevator, rings for it, talking without a pause. "Gee, we really are going to give great consideration to your premise. The ideas are wonderful. How nice of you to bring them in. We were going to use them as a door stop, but we decided to give them back to you."

The elevator arrives, crammed with people. He keeps the elevator door open as he continues to blabber on. Wonderful ad-libs, I must say, in retrospect.

The next thing I know, he nudges me onto the elevator. The doors close. I'm down on the ground floor. I'm out on the street, and I'm standing there, quivering. The perspiration just rolling down my face. My body is drenched. That was the last time I ever went to ABC. I couldn't go back, I was so humiliated.

Several years pass. I move out to the west coast and my agent Marty Shapiro sets up a pitch meeting at 20th Century-Fox, with an important executive who is still active and shall remain nameless.

I go to the studio. I get there at least an hour early for my meeting. I do not want to be late. The guard at the gate-house does not have my name on the list.

So, again. I'm totally embarrassed. He calls upstairs and they say, "Mr. Rotcop is an hour early and we haven't yet called down his name. Tell him he is going to have to wait at the gate until we can get the pass down."

I am holding up a line of about a zillion cars, all waiting to go to work. I am told to move over to the sidelines so I can let the cars on the lot.

An eternity later, when the pass comes, the guard says to me, "You got forty-five minutes, what are you going to do?" I say, "I've never been on a lot before, I'll walk around. Where's the commissary? I may have a cup of tea. Where's the, ah, gift shop? Maybe I'll pick up something for my wife."

Finally, I'm ushered into the executive's office and I swear he is sitting at a desk on a platform. I'm sitting on a chair below the platform looking up at him. He is also sitting with the window at his back; the sun is glaring in, so I'm squinting at him. I'm feeling like I'm two feet tall because he's hovering over me like some God from another dimension, and he says, "Yes, what can I do for you?"

"What can I do for you?" He knew we had a meeting. He knew I was there to pitch something. Why did he ask me that question like "I don't even know why you're here!" He knew damn well why I was here.

"I'm here to pitch an idea for a screenplay."

"Fine, I'd like to listen to it, but wait a second." He calls his secretary in and says, "Bring me the letters to sign." She comes in with a stack of papers, and he says to me, "Go ahead, let's hear your pitch."

His head is down; he's signing these letters. I'm looking up at him, squinting into the sun. I start my pitch to the top of his head, because I cannot see his face, which is buried in these letters he's signing. I'm wondering if he's even listening to me.

Now, part way through my pitch the phone rings. His secretary buzzes the intercom with, "It's your wife on line four." "Excuse me," he says, and swivels his chair completely around away from me and starts to talk to his wife on the phone. The conversation goes on for about ten minutes. She is giving him a list of items to pick up at the grocery store because they are having some guests over that night.

After that conversation, he swivels back and says, "Now where were we?"

"Why don't I start over from the beginning?"

"No, no, no, pick it up from where we were, but tell me where you are in the story."

I am now totally lost. I'm confused. What should I tell him? What did I already tell him? I couldn't remember, but tried to pick up the pieces. I'm just about to proceed, when he stops me. "Hold on one second."

He buzzes his secretary. "Have the trades come in yet?"

"Yes, they have."

"Please bring them in."

In comes the *Hollywood Reporter* and *Daily Variety*. He hands her the pile of letters that he's now signed, and says to me, "Go on, continue." As I'm continuing, he's reading the trade papers.

When I finally finish, there is a painfully long silence. All of a sudden he looks up and says, "Are you done?"

"Yes, I am."

"Is there anything else you want to pitch?"

"No."

"Thank you very much for coming in."

"Are you interested in the story?"

"I'll talk to your agent."

Neither my agent nor I ever hear from him.

The years go by, and now I have a certain status in the industry. Another meeting is set up with this same executive. I go to his office. This time it's a different office, but with same platform. He has it built the same way, and starts to pull the same crap on me. I say, "Stop writing those letters and listen to me."

He is shocked, but he puts the pen down. He says, "Go ahead."

"No. I'm not going to start until I have your attention."

He starts to bluster something, and then says "Go ahead."

The phone rings. I blurt out, "Don't answer that phone! You set up this meeting with me, and damn it, I expect to have your full attention!"

He does not pick up the phone. And I say, "And one more thing, get down from your desk and come over and sit next to me so I don't have to squint into the sun."

He does so.

I finish the pitch. He says, "I'll be in touch."

I leave the office feeling ten feet tall.

He never calls my agent. He never calls me.

Those were just three of my experiences. I've had others that were worse!

Pitching sucks!

But let me show you how to make it work.

WHAT WORKS FOR ME
The Rotcop Touch.

Overheard at the Workshop:

"I could tell the producer was really getting into my pitch. Who doesn't like to hear about drugs, group sex and rock and roll? He even knew the band's music. And as I'm winding up the story, he says, 'tell me about the protagonist's character arc. How does he change at the end?' 'Well, he doesn't do as many drugs,' I replied."

I have listened to over one thousand pitches in my lifetime. I've probably given a couple of hundred. I've been Creative Head of four studios, and have literally had a parade of writers, directors, producers, and executives come to my numerous offices to pitch and pitch and pitch, yet again.

As a writer, I've gone to every studio and to most production companies and to cocktail parties and ball games, anyplace where I could get the ear of somebody who might be of some influence, and I'd pitch and pitch and pitch, yet again.

Spend a week in Hollywood and you will hear a zillion pitches whether you're in the industry or not. Everybody in town has a story, everybody likes to pitch.

I have found that the best pitches take no more than two minutes. A pitch is a two-minute commercial. If they can sell millions of widgets in a one-minute commercial on television, why in the world can't you convince an executive to read your script in *two minutes*?

A pitch screams out, between the lines, "Read my script. Read my script. Please, please read my script."

And on the other hand, the screenplay itself, between those lines, screams out, "Buy me, buy me, buy me. I will make you a lot of money, I promise you."

When you sit down to pitch a script, the very first thing you want to do is make eye contact with the executive. Next, tell him the name of the script and the genre. In other words, whether it is action-adventure or comedy or drama. Then, let him know if it is for a feature film or a Movie of the Week (MOW) for television. Then, if you have representation, give him the name of your agent, manager, or entertainment attorney.

Many executives have a million things on their mind when you sit down to pitch. They may be thinking about another pitch they've heard that day that was terrific, and in their minds, they're deciding how to cast it. They may be thinking about a movie they saw the night before that they wish they had made. Or, they may just be thinking about what they want to have for lunch. So, what you must do immediately is grab their attention.

Two examples of something that I might use to get their attention are: 1) Ask them a question that has to do with the script. For instance, for my screenplay, *Red Mafia*, I might ask them how much they know about the Russian Mafia and how it affects their lives.

This will immediately grab their attention as they start to think of an answer to your question. They may know a great deal about the Russian Mafia and they might go on for a number of minutes talking about it. That's wonderful, you're now having them involved in a script which you haven't even started to pitch yet.

On the other hand, they might say, "I don't know anything about the Russian Mafia," which is fine too, because again, they've stopped to think about your script. They've taken everything else that was on their mind and put it in the background.

So it doesn't matter whether they answer your question "yes" or if the answer is "no." What you've done is taken them away from whatever they were thinking about before you walked in and now they can hone in on you. By asking them a question, you've gotten them involved.

2) The second thing I do before I start my pitch is try to find an j.

During my visit, there was a party for all the people who had ever lived there. We all sat around having dinner, meeting new people, catching up with former housemates and sharing a smoke or two.

There was a swimming pool at this house, and after dinner we all went in and stood there holding hands around the perimeter of the pool. Somebody from the far side of the pool yelled at me, "Hey, Rotcop, you're a writer, I'm charging you with the responsibility of writing about this house."

You see, this building was a halfway house for divorced people. I lived there when I split with my wife. While I'd gone through numerous adventures there, I had never once thought about the possibility of writing a screenplay until this guy on the other side of the pool yelled out at me, "Hey, Rotcop, write about the house." So I did and was able to sell that script to Tri-Star.

I find that when I tell that story, I immediately get the executive's interest, and he can hardly wait for the pitch.

So, those are the two systems that I use. One, ask a question that has to do with your script to get their attention. Two, tell an interesting story of why or how you wrote the script. You will find that you now have their undivided attention.
The pitch itself should be no longer than two minutes. After two minutes, you're going to start to lose their attention. You may notice their eyes glazing over. You may notice a leg begins to shake. Or, they may start to reach for certain things on their desk, sometimes even just straightening the desk out. These are all hints that you've gone about as far as you can with that

pitch. My old boss, Joseph E. Levine, would take off his wristwatch and place it on the desk. You knew it was time to end the pitch.

Let them know the pitch is over by saying, "Would you like to read my script?" That tells them you're finished. Or you could ask, "Do you have any questions?" or "Is there anything more I can tell you about my story?"

If they liked what they've heard, they will start to ask you a lot of questions. Questions are good, because no one knows the story better than you. Questions are easier to answer than pitching the story.

They might ask you about casting. They might ask what the budget might be for the script. They might ask you about locations. They might ask you a lot of questions that you cannot answer.

Be honest. Tell them, "I'm not prepared to answer that question for you. I don't know who would make good casting. I don't know what a good budget would be. I have no idea where this picture should be shot." Don't worry about those answers. Better to be honest with them than to try to create suggestions on the spur of the moment.

In fact, they may be testing you. They really don't care who you would like to see cast in the movie. They know you don't have any concept of budget. After all, you're a writer, not a production manager. Thirdly, as far as location is concerned, who cares where *you* want to shoot it? You may want to shoot it in Sydney, Australia. They may want to shoot it in your backyard.

They're asking these questions for a particular reason — to see if you are somebody they can work with. In other words, when you pitch a story, you are being judged in two areas. One, how good is the story, and, two, is this somebody they want to work with? The questions could even get more preposterous: Do you have a spouse? What did he or she think of the script? Or, gee, I love the story about these cowboys in the West, but could you make them gnomes instead? They're testing you. They want to see how you respond.

They might also ask what other companies have seen the script. You must be honest and tell them so they don't duplicate submissions. They may ask you who has turned down the script. Do not bad-mouth any of the companies. Don't say, "Damn that MGM. I thought I had a deal there, but they're so stupid, they turned it down at the last minute."

The executive you're pitching to is going to think to himself, "If you're bad-mouthing MGM today, you could be bad-mouthing me tomorrow. Since Hollywood is a relatively small community, I don't need to work with somebody who is walking around with a chip on their shoulder."

You could actually lose a deal. Believe me, I've known a number of deals that have been blown where the executive loved the material, but disliked the writer. Don't come across as a malcontent.

When you pitch, you must bring two elements to the pitch: enthusiasm and passion. Be enthusiastic about your pitch. Let the executive know how lucky he is that you have come to him to share your story. Make him feel that this is the highlight of his day, and boy, he should hang onto every word because you're about to bring him fame and fortune. Enthusiasm while you pitch is very important.

The second thing is passion. You must be passionate about your story. Don't let them derail you by watering down your passion.

I know one executive who, when he wants to say no to a pitch, instead says, after the writer has pitched the story, "Who cares about these people? Why would anybody waste eight dollars to spend two hours with these people who nobody is going to care about?"
You have just been rejected. You must fight for your story. You must convince that executive that people will care, that this story is important, that there are thousands and thousands of people out there who have gone through similar experiences or who will be curious to share that experience.

Even if he rejects your pitch, he will admire you for being passionate about your story. And, I guarantee you, he'll say to you, "When you have another project, please call because I love your passion."

Don't be afraid of screwing up. When I first started in the business, at one of the first meetings I took, the executive asked me a question, which I've since blocked out after all these years, but I gave an answer. As I was giving it, I said to myself, "This is the most stupid thing I have ever said. I can't believe these words are coming out of my mouth. I can't believe I'm actually saying this. He must think I'm the biggest jerk in the world. Oh my God, I can't stop now, I've got to complete these sentences."

When I left the office, I remember walking into the hallway and banging my forehead against the wall, and yelling out for anyone to hear, "Stupid, stupid, stupid. Oh, did I blow that meeting, what a jerk I am."

I probably did that two or three times in the early years of my career. Moronic things come out when you're nervous, when you're so desperate to make a deal, when you're trying so hard to be liked and appreciated. Stupid things come out of your mouth. It happens all the time.

How do I know it happens all the time? Because a number of years later, when I was Creative Head of a studio, I must have had phone calls from five different writers within a one-year period who said something to the effect of, "Mr. Rotcop, I met with you two days ago and I said something so stupid, I've been beating myself and punishing myself ever since. So I had to call you and apologize for the stupid thing I said. You must think I'm an idiot."

In truth, number one, I didn't remember what they said that was so stupid. Number two, I probably couldn't even remember them! Number three, all I cared about was their story. Number four, if they came across as people that I couldn't work with, then it didn't matter what they said, because I wasn't going to use them anyway.

Try to remember that within one week executives will see writer after writer after director after producer, so it's not at all unusual for an executive to get 20 to 25 pitches in that time frame. In a good month, I could hear close to 100 different pitches.

If you think executives remember something stupid that you've said, trust me, they don't. It's what we call the Gestalt theory, which means they get a holistic view of the writer. They get an impression, an overview of who you are. You may hang on every word, but, I promise you, they don't.

Stop worrying about saying something idiotic. As a matter of fact, what you think is stupid, they may think is brilliant.

Screenwriters have to pitch. Television episodic writers have to pitch. Only the poet, the novelist and the playwright don't have to pitch. If you hate pitching, I suggest you become a poet, a novelist or a playwright.

Without a doubt the easiest pitches to make are based on action stories, horror movies, thrillers, science fiction, action-adventure, and fantasy. Tougher pitches are romantic comedies or character-driven stories that depend on characterization and dialogue. These are called "soft stories."

Soft stories don't usually generate much visual excitement, and are much more difficult to pitch. If you have that kind of story, you better damn well practice your pitch. Make it as interesting as you can because you don't have the car chases or ghosts coming out of the walls. You don't have people with guns shooting at each other. You don't have earthquakes, firestorms, tornadoes, or violent destruction to fall back on.
If you have a romantic comedy, or a people-driven story, you must work on your pitch to make it as exciting as a roller coaster. We'll go into the "soft" pitch in a later chapter.

In the next chapter, I'm going to give you a quiz. Get out your pencil and paper. I promise you nobody ever fails this test and most important, hopefully, you will learn something from it.

A QUIZ YOU CANNOT FAIL
A Quiz for Pitching Your Script.

Overheard at the Workshop:

"I was so naive; this guy loves my pitch and asks, 'How does five-thousand for the option sound?' And I say, 'Give me six weeks to raise it.' And he says, 'No, no, we pay you!'"

I can hear you saying, "What, a quiz already?" I think this test is a good learning tool and I suspect you'll have some fun with it too!

1. You can either see the head honcho of a production company for five minutes or you can see his story editor for an hour. Which one would you chose?

In other words, you call for an appointment and you are told the top executive has a lot going for him that day, but he can see you for five minutes or you can meet with the story editor and spend an hour with him. Which one would you choose?

2. You have two ideas, one is excellent, the other is very good. Which one do you start with at the pitch meeting?

3. The producer likes your story, likes your pitch, but says he has a very good writer in mind to do the screenplay. What do you do?

4. In the middle of the pitch, the executive tells you the company has a similar project in development. Should you continue your story or should you stop? Should you say, "Wait a minute, listen to the rest of my story before you make up your mind?" Or should you say, "Thank you very much" and stop right there?

5. The producer asks for "five or six pages." Should you insist he pay you for that?

6. You're presenting a story idea to a busy producer who keeps interrupting your pitch to answer his phone. Should you, (a) be patient, (b) tell him you'll come back another time, or (c) ask him not to take calls during your presentation? (If you read our preamble, you might have gotten a hint how to handle this one.)

7. You read a hot story in a newspaper or a magazine. Should you immediately do a fictionalized version or try to get the rights to the story?

8. A producer loves your story, loves your pitch, options it after he's read the script, then asks you to make changes you don't believe in. Do you, (a) fight him, (b) make the changes quietly or (c) walk away from the project?

Now, let's go over the answers.

1. You can either see the top executive for five minutes or a story editor for an hour. Always go to the head man, even if it's only for five minutes. He's the one who makes the final decision.

If you go to a story editor, even if he loves your story, you're at his mercy to tell the story as well as you did to his boss. I have also found that when I've chosen to talk to the top guy, if he really loves my idea, it's amazing how suddenly he'll find an hour to discuss the project.

2. You have two ideas, one is excellent, the other is very good, which do you start with? Always go with your best, go with the one you feel is excellent, make that deal. If they subsequently ask you what else you have to pitch, don't pitch anything else, just the one they want to make the deal on.

Tell them after the deal is made, you'll come back with another idea. Don't dilute your material, if you already have them interested in one. Don't be a pig and try to walk out with two deals. Nobody in the history of the industry has ever walked out of a meeting with two deals. Thank the Lord that you've made one.

3. The producer wants your story but wants someone else to write the script. What do you do? Well, it depends on your situation. If you believe in your story more than anything, if this is your baby, tell him you'll come back after you've written your script and you'll give him another look at it.

If, on the other hand, this is just a good idea that you've come up with, but you have other projects you want to work on, and he wants to make a deal to option or buy your story, and give it to somebody else to write the screenplay, then make the deal and move on.

Just remember this, the person who writes the screenplay gets a fee ten to twenty times greater than the person who came up with the story.

4. In the middle of a pitch, the executive tells you he has a similar project in development. Should you continue your story or stop?

You stop. When they tell you they have something similar, it means one of two things. Either, one, he hates your story but he doesn't know how to go about telling you he hates it, or two, he really does have something in development that's similar.

If they have something in development that's similar, why in the world would you give them your ideas which they'll incorporate in their story? Stop the minute he says he has something similar.

5. The producer likes your story and asks for five to six pages. The Writers Guild of America frowns on this, but the answer is a series of "if's." If you're not a member of the Writers Guild, and if you're anxious

11

to make your first deal, and if you like the producer and he looks like he can get this project made, then I would suggest, as a first-time writer, you should go ahead and write those pages. Give him some ammunition that he can use to sell your project.

On the other hand, if you feel that he's asking too much, see if you can negotiate it down to one or two pages. If, however, you don't want to give him any material, then don't. Again, it depends on your own personal and financial situation.

6. You present a story to a busy producer who keeps interrupting your pitch.

If you go back to the book's preface, you'll know how I eventually learned to handle that. But I must say, when I first started out, it would not have been easy for me to talk back to the executive and start making certain demands of my own.

But should you: (a) be patient? Possibly, yes. (b) Should you tell him you'll come back another time? Absolutely not. If a meeting has been set up, that time has supposedly been allotted to you to pitch your story and for the executive to ask questions about it. Never tell him you'll come back another time. (c) Ask him not to take calls during your presentation. I do that now, but I've been in the business thirty-three years. I had to win awards before I got the gumption to say to them, "Put that phone down and listen to what I have to say." Again, I leave that final answer up to you.

7. You've read a hot story in a newspaper or magazine. Should you change it, do a fictionalized version, or go immediately in and pitch it to an executive?

The answer is "no." Forget it! If there's a hot story in a newspaper or magazine, I can guarantee all the studios are on it, as well as all the major production companies. They already immediately contacted the people involved to get options to the rights to the story.

For you to come in and pitch a "hot" story that you've read is a waste of time. They're not going to be interested in doing business with you, particularly since you will not have the rights to the story.

However, that doesn't mean newspapers and magazines are not good sources for material. On the contrary, they're excellent sources. Just go back to old issues of these periodicals that have been around for a number of years and pluck material out of them. In those cases, you probably don't even need the rights, particularly if the articles are about people who are not famous, names that are not easily recognizable. You can pitch those stories and you can even fictionalize them. None of the original people is likely to ever know about it or have any claim to your story.

8. The producer loves your story and he options it from you. Then, he asks you to make changes that you don't believe in. Well, that's a tough one, because the minute it's optioned, whether he gave you a dollar or ten thousand dollars, he now owns your material and you are employed by him.

Let's explore the possibilities. Do you fight him? Yes, if you passionately believe that the changes are not to the benefit of the script. Sure, take a stand, and say, "I'm not going to make these changes, I don't believe in them." Maybe he'll back down.

Should you make the changes quietly? Well, I don't think you should make them quietly. You can say to him, "Look, I'll try it your way, but I don't think it's going to work. But I will make the best effort to do the scenes the way you would like me to do them, and then we can look them over and see if they still work."

Or should you walk away from the project? Again, it all depends on what your financial situation is. I do not know a lot of writers who can walk away from a project. Plus, you can get a bad rep for being a quitter.

This is what usually happens: First, you fight him, then you end up making the changes. I've even known of a few cases — not many — a

13

few, where the writer ended up thanking the producer for the idea because it did, in fact, turn out better than what the writer originally had.

CREATING THE PITCHMART
An Idea Whose Time Has Come.

Overheard at the Workshop:

"I'm half-way to the studio to pitch to a big-shot producer when I panic! I stop the car, call his secretary on my cell phone and cancel the meeting, telling her I have a combination of flu, whooping cough, and measles. And she says, 'Call us again when you get over your panic attack.'"

One recent change in the movie industry is the mass pitch session, where executives from studios and production companies gather to meet with emerging writers to hear their pitches. I know from personal experiences there were numerous deals made through these pitch sessions.

In this chapter I'm going to tell you how this all started and about the success that the Professional Writers Workshop has had with their pitch sessions. Also, how you can get to a pitch session so you can pitch your script to executives.

In 1985, I was invited to teach a course on screenwriting at UCLA in the extension division. Somewhat to my surprise, I discovered that in a class of twenty students, there must have been a dozen really good screenplays.

I found the problem with these new writers, who were my students, was not that they were unable to come up with stories and put them down in a professional manner. They didn't know how to break that invisible bubble called the "mystique of Hollywood." It was a case of "I've got my script, now what the hell do I do with it?" As the teacher of this class, I thought it only fitting that I find a way to help them sell their scripts.

First, I discussed it with my literary agent. He said the last thing he wanted was to read screenplays by first-time writers. He told me that each week he was inundated with new writer inquiries. He simply wasn't staffed to take on novices. Within a year, he would get well over a hundred inquiries from wannabes, new writers who wanted to submit their screenplays. He compared it to searching for a needle in a haystack.

He just wasn't interested in representing my writers. To his credit, he relented — a little bit. "Okay, pick out one or two of the best and I'll read those." That was great, but it wasn't solving my problem. How do I get a dozen good scripts exposed to top executives in the industry?

Instead, when their scripts were ready, I had my agent set up meetings for me! On an average day, I would meet four to six executives, who thought I was pitching my own material, when in reality I was talking about screenplays written by my students.

Because the studios and production companies are spread all over Los Angeles, I was hopping from North Hollywood in the San Fernando Valley to Santa Monica near the ocean, then back to the Valley, then off to Culver City, south of LA on the way to the airport. All the while with a pack on my back peddling scripts from my UCLA class.

As much as I hated the idea, I found myself saying to executives, "Here's one script. If you don't like this one, here's another. If you don't like this one, here's a third, and after that, I've got a fourth and a fifth." Still, that's exactly what I did. I was going around with these screenplays in a backpack. My back was bent so low I felt like Santa Claus with a bag full of goodies. But instead of going to good little boys and girls, I was trying to sell them to big, stern executives. It just didn't seem to be working out.

I knew there must be a better way, but at the time, I couldn't figure out what it was.

One day, my wife invited me to go with her to a flea market. You must understand, any invitation from my wife is a subtle order, a command so to speak. So off I went.

It was held in this huge warehouse filled with little booths in which dozens and dozens of merchants were selling different kinds of merchandise. The shoppers were literally going from one booth to the next. I thought to myself, "Instead of going around with this pack on my back, why can't I bring all the executives to one huge room, give them each their own 'booths' and let the writers, like the shoppers at the flea market, go from booth to booth trying to sell their screenplays?" Perhaps they could convince these executives to read their scripts with the hope that sales would be made down the road.

In 1985, I decided to try out the new concept at Pierce College, a small community college in the San Fernando Valley where I also taught. We invited two executives and two agents. I literally stationed each one in a different corner of the classroom. All they needed were a stool and a dunce cap to look like the class dunce.

One executive was Bob Kosberg who is currently with Merv Griffith Productions. The other was Ron Jacobs, who at the time was with PM Films and 40 Love Productions. The two agents were Tracy Washington with the Leslie Parness Agency and Jackie Thompson of Quillco Literary Agency. Voila. With two agents and two executives, the first "Pitchmart" was created.

In that classroom in 1985, my twenty-five students each got a chance to go from corner to corner meeting individually with these four people, either pitching their scripts in hopes of getting an agent to represent them or an executive to purchase their story.

It was such a success, we decided to try it again six months later. I invited more executives and moved it out of Pierce College. They didn't have a room with more corners, so we got ourselves a hall with lots of tables. We've been doing it ever since. Every six months. With more than two dozen executives at each Pitchmart.

In the beginning, I called in every favor I had to get executives to come. They didn't know what I was talking about when I said, "Pitchmart."

They didn't understand that they would be meeting all these writers, one on one. Many of them prepared speeches, thinking they were going to be speaking before the group. Some of them flaked out and never showed. Some sent minor executives to replace them at the last minute. Some even sent their office boy to sit in for them. Because they didn't know what they were coming to, they were either confused, terrified of new writers, or they considered it a waste of time. They thought there would be a mass run of wannabe writers, and many of them chickened out at the last minute.

But something began to happen. After the first few Pitchmarts, word began to spread through the motion picture community. "There's this guy, Rotcop, who has very good writers, who have completed screenplays that have been revised and polished in his class." I told them, "The story may not be right for you, but I guarantee the scripts are commercial and you'll know you've read a professionally written script."

Suddenly, the phone was ringing off the hook. It reached a point where it got too much for me to handle. People wanted to know, "When is the next Pitchmart?" and "Why wasn't my name on the last list?" and "What do I have to do to get to this one?" Or, "Give me a list of people who are coming, I only want to come if I can be exclusive." Those were among the problems we were facing. Also, "How can I be guaranteed a good table?" or "I only want to meet with writers who have good scripts!" Duh.

Sometimes at these Pitchmarts, I would say to the executives, "All those who want to read bad scripts raise your hand." I've never had anybody raise their hand yet.

So that's how we started the Pitchmart. It really became successful. We started making deals, optioning scripts, selling screenplays. Writers were calling me. Executives were calling me.

What I did next was start private workshops with many of the students from my classes at UCLA and Pierce that were staying with me. We set up workshops all over the San Fernando Valley and Santa Monica.

In the beginning, we would have Pitchmarts twice a year — in the Spring and Fall. They became so successful that a number of people who were invited decided to go off on their own to start their own pitch sessions. I had to register the word "Pitchmart" so that no one else could use it and denigrate the quality of what we have.

There are now a number of other pitch sessions around town. What follows are the ones I would recommend. Find out when they are being held, and in one swoop, one day of your life, you can meet anywhere from ten to fifteen executives who will listen to your pitch. And if you've done a good job, they will read your script. And if they read your script and buy it, well....

"LET'S DO LUNCH"   (818) 594-4144

This excellent program is more like the "setup of a relationship" rather than a pitch session. One producer/executive has lunch with approximately eight people. Then, at dessert, a different producer/executive moves to your table. You discuss your career, scripts, etc. It's more informal than at a pitch session, and you get lunch. Also it's the least expensive. Five sessions or lunches with the executive are just $59. A great way to make contacts.

SHERWOOD OAKS EXPERIMENTAL COLLEGE
(323) 851-7169

GARY SHUSETT puts on a variety of events each year, including a Producer/Executive Seminar with a pitch session. He has a unique week-long program where you go to a different studio each day and executives come to discuss their needs, etc. It's relationship, rather than pitch-oriented, but still an excellent program. Call and get on his mailing list.

HOLLYWOOD PITCH FESTIVAL   (800) 646-3896

I've heard they are one of the best. Four sessions over two days. I spoke to two men who each pitched to over thirty executives. Call for details.

SPEC SCRIPT MARKETPLACE   **(310) 396-1662**
EVA PEEL has many pitch sessions and an Agents and Managers pitch session each year. It is very well respected.

Now the original Pitchmart™ (the one I started that has been covered by the *Los Angeles Times*, the *Wall Street Journal*, and papers as far away as the *Manila Times*, plus sundry other show biz magazines) is open only to members of my Workshop. These people have developed their material in the Workshop and their scripts must get my stamp of approval before they can be pitched at our Pitchmarts.

If you're interested in joining my Workshop as a correspondent or in person in the Greater Los Angeles area, call (818) 883-0554.

You do not have to be a member of any writing group in order to register for these other pitch sessions. But because these executives are listening to wannabe writers who may not have formal training, they tend to be tougher, so you're going to have to knock their socks off to get them to read your material.

I understand from executives who have gone to these other pitch sessions, there is a dearth of professionally written material, because so many people have had no training at all. If you've read this book and you practice what you've learned in it, you should stand out from the crowd and have a much better chance of having your scripts read.

As for the Pitchmart, I've actually lost count of how many movies have resulted from these sessions. It is certainly more than a dozen, probably around 15 or 16, and that list continues to grow with each Pitchmart we have.

We've also had 80 or 90 screenplays optioned over the years, and numerous writers have received writing assignments from different executives. How many have gotten assignments? We've simply lost count. Also, many of the writers who started their careers in the

Workshop have gone off on their own and have been very successful in getting pictures made.

These writers still give credit to the Professional Writers Workshop as the place where they learned the "secrets of the trade." Writers from the Workshop regularly invite me to cast and crew screenings of feature films, movies for television or direct-to-videos they've completed. I'm as proud of my students as any father watching his child take a first step!

ROTCOP'S KEY QUESTIONS
What Studio Readers Will Ask.

Overheard at the Workshop:

"I'm thirty seconds into my pitch and I go blank. Absolutely forget everything. So he finishes the story. He pitches his version of my story to me! When he's done I say, 'So what do you think?' And he says, 'I hate it!'"

The following are the key questions a professional reader will ask about your script.

1. What is the Concept, Premise, or Hook?
2. Whose Story Is It? Who Do We Root for?
3. How Does the Lead Character Change over the Course of the Script?
4. Does Each Scene Advance the Story?
5. Stories are about People. Do We Care What Happens to Your People?
6. Is Your Idea Fresh, Unique or an Exciting New Twist on a Familiar Story, Arena, or Genre?
7. Is Your Story Castable? Are There Roles that Actors Will Be Eager to Play?

If you can't answer these questions in a pitch session, what docs that say about your script?

GIMMICKS AND PROPS
Taking Visuals to the Pitch Meeting.

Overheard at the Workshop:

"I get a pitch meeting, but no ideas. So I tell the producer, 'My dog ate my script.' 'Go on,' he says. 'Since he's a talking dog, I send him in to do the pitch. Next thing I know he's writing himself into the story.' The producer says, 'Stop! I love it!' And that's how I made my first deal!"

Often when you pitch, you can use a prop, gimmick or resume to aid in selling the concept.

I remember selling a magic show to one of the networks. The program was going to be the first annual magic awards, which were to be called "The Eric Awards" after Eric Weiss who, when he came to this country from Europe, changed his name to Harry Houdini.

When I pitched the project to the network, I took along two props and a gimmick. The first was a bunch of 8 x 10 glossies of the magicians who were going to be competing.

My second prop, a poster, was based on the fact that the show was going to be performed for a black-tie audience, with the ticket proceeds going to a fund for a crippling children's disease. It was a beautiful poster with the slogan, "Nimble Fingers Work So Tiny Feet Can Walk."

Now for the gimmick. Just a week before I was to make my pitch to the network, I went into a trophy store and told the proprietor about my magic show. "What do you have that would work for the Eric Awards?" I asked. "Let me show you something I have in the back," he answered, and brought out an unusual trophy. It had never been used and it was the most distinctive thing I had ever seen. "It's perfect! Make one up that says 'Eric Awards' on it."

I picked it up on the day of the meeting. I didn't even open the box, just rushed off to the network. There were six executives in the room and I made my verbal pitch. I showed them the glossies and then the poster. I kept the pitch under two minutes. And all they said was, "What's in the box?"

I proceeded to cut the tape, and open the box, and I pull out this trophy with a marble base supporting a plastic cylinder that was filled with some kind of liquid. Floating up and down in the liquid was a coin with Houdini's likeness on it. "Gentlemen," I proclaimed, "the Eric Award." They were mesmerized.

First one executive said, "I've got to have one of those for my desk."

Another said, "Me, too, order one for me." Before I knew it, all six of them wanted an Eric Award for their desk or trophy shelf. I had sold them on two props and a gimmick. They bought the show on the trophy more than anything I said or showed them during the pitch.

Some of the screenwriters from my Writers Workshop have come up with terrific gimmicks.

One fellow cuts out pictures of men and women from magazines. When he goes to pitch his script, he says, "This is the story of Sam Brown the architect." Then he takes out a photo of a man and puts it down in front of the executives.

The executive now sees what Sam Brown looks like. Sam Brown is in love with Mary White. He puts the picture of a beautiful model down next to Sam Brown. That's Mary White. Very jealous of both of them is Henry Black. He puts down a picture of a guy who looks villainous. Now the executive sees what the antagonist looks like.

This really works when there are a lot of characters in your pitch. Without the visuals, it's guaranteed both the executive *and even you* will get confused about who is who.

It's an instant visual aid that has been very, very successful.

A woman writer in my Workshop went through the horrible, disastrous fire at the MGM Grand in Las Vegas that took many lives.

She and her husband were there in the hotel when the fire erupted. They were on the 17th floor and literally walked over bodies in the hallway to get to the elevator. When the elevator stopped at their floor, it was jammed with people. They were just about to squeeze on, when the husband read the notice that said, **In case of fire use stairwell, do not use the elevator.**

He said, "We should not be taking this elevator." His wife insisted, "Let's get on it, there's smoke all around us!" "No, we're going to take the stairwell." The elevator closed and they've had nightmares ever since because they never knew if that elevator ever made it down to the lobby or not.

As she tells this story of their escape, she shows photos of that horrendous fire. She shows one picture after another, photos of the fire from newspapers and magazines. She draws the executives in, to the point where it becomes so compelling, they cannot say no to her story.

There have been other gimmicks. One of my writers went to a five-and-dime store and bought little toy figures. Her toy soldiers, her toy football player, and her toy truck all play an integral part in her pitch.

One of my female writers wrote a screenplay about the first pregnant superhero. The writer came to the pitch with a cape and padding around her waist. She hasn't sold that script yet, but people do say her pitch is an attention-grabber!

One writer had a video presentation machine and ran 8mm home movies of his kids playing the parts of the characters in his story. The play-acting was cute and captivating to the executives and they found it very effective.

Another writer whose story took place in an exotic location, thought to go to a travel agency, and picked up a bunch of posters of those particular locations, using those to set the scene for his pitch. That, too, was very effective.

One of our hip young writers, who wrote a story about hip young people, came to his pitch wearing very sharp, yuppie, wrap-around *Men In Black* sunglasses. I don't know how effective that gimmick was, since he hasn't sold his script yet, but we all got a good laugh.

A gimmick is anything that would enhance the communication, the concise, but engaging, telling of your story. Anything that would make it easier for the executive to visualize your screenplay. The gimmick should not be obtrusive though. The pitch should not become so dependent upon the gimmick that the story gets lost.

For instance, in the case of the magic show, had I pulled out that very unusual trophy first, before I made my pitch, I doubt whether they would have even listened to the pitch. A gimmick should *supplement* the pitch, not take over the pitch. And it should be presented at the most appropriate part of your meeting. Sometimes during, and sometimes, like a punchline, at the end.

Another item in the same vein as a gimmick is the use of a resume. When is it appropriate and when is it not?

I don't feel using a resume is a good gimmick unless your background is filled with movies or television shows or even plays that you've actually had produced.

A resume should list what qualifies you to be an expert, or at least knowledgeable on the material you're pitching. Of course, if you've written a script about the CIA in Ecuador, and in fact, you were a member of the CIA in Ecuador, that would be worth sharing. On the other hand, if all you knew about the CIA in Ecuador is what you read in a book, I'm afraid having that put on a resume would not be advantageous.

If you sold plumbing your whole life and your script is about a love affair between an astronaut and an alien, I don't think selling plumbing is going to impress the executive. You're better off not handing in a resume in that case.

So if you want to submit a resume with your pitch, make sure everything you put on it is relevant to your story.

Remember, a resume is only a good gimmick if it enhances your credibility.

I know a writer who makes a list of all the scripts he's written, along with a thumbnail description of each. Then he asks the executive to pick out which pitch he'd like to hear. A list of everything you've written that has not been sold only indicates to the executive that you've had a lot of rejections. In fact, he would probably think, "If no one else wants your script, why should I?" Don't bring out a "laundry list" of unsold screenplays and ask the executive to pick the one he'd like you to pitch. That's a gimmick that's going to backfire.

Bring in the clowns and the dancing girls, whatever props, gimmicks, and resumes it takes to enhance your pitch. Just make sure they are appropriate to your screenplay. You may dazzle 'em but, bottom line, you'll only sell 'em if your story works.

FIFTEEN TIPS FOR BEGINNERS
Fifteen Key Points for Wannabe Writers.

Overheard at the Workshop:

"I'm sitting in a stall in the men's room at this studio when someone comes into the one next to mine. 'Hey, Charlie,' he says to me, 'Wanna hear my story now?' I'm not Charlie, but I say, 'Sure.' He proceeds to pitch this god-awful story, then, as he flushes asks, 'So what do you think?' And I answer, 'I hope that was your story going down the toilet!'"

1. Always grab the reader by page 3. By page 10, we should know who the protagonist is, what his goal is and who or what is stopping him from reaching it!
2. Use colorful, dynamic descriptions:
    He *walked* to his car. Boring! Make it: he runs, races, speeds, jumps, staggers, falls into, bolts for.... Get the idea?
3. Forget camera angles. You are the storyteller, not the director.
4. Read scripts! See movies! (Many services in Hollywood and on the Internet sell scripts.) Rent videos of feature films and follow along with the screenplay.
5. The three key books: Lajos Egri's *The Art of Dramatic Writing*. William Goldman's *Adventures in the Screen Trade*. Jason Squire's *The Movie Business*.
6. Writing is rewriting! And rewriting and rewriting.
7. Make sure we can root for the protagonist.
8. What does he learn? How does he grow?
9. Keep the script between 95 and 120 pages. The thinner the script the better chance it has to be read.
10. No food stains, turned-down pages or notes in the margins when sending out your screenplay.
11. Happy ending = Audience satisfied.

12. Write contemporary stories only. It's very, very tough to sell a costume or period piece the first time out.
13. Do not send out step outlines, presentations or treatments. Full screenplays only! It's the only way they can tell if you can write.
14. Ask yourself this: Is my screenplay as exciting as a roller coaster ride?
15. Scripts are not about events, scripts are about people. Sometimes the event will have an impact on the characters. Other times the characters will have an impact on the event. But the characters always come first!

PITCHING AS A PERFORMANCE
The Performer's Edge: Overcoming the Fear of Pitching.
By James Shea

Overheard at the Workshop:

"There I was in the middle of my pitch when I realized the producer had fallen asleep. I wasn't sure what to do, but I learned in the Workshop: Plow ahead! So I finished my pitch to the snoring executive. All was silent for a minute or two, when he jerks his head and wakes up. 'Now where were we?' he asked. I said, 'You were just about to give me a contract.' 'Of course,' he replied, calling in his secretary with the paperwork. And that's how I optioned my first screenplay."

I have often told writers that to broaden their writing horizons and also to help them pitch better, they should take acting lessons. As a writer, it will clearly show you what an "actable" is. Something that can be acted, as opposed to "unactable" like "He blanches white." It sounds okay, but try to act it.

Also, just a little bit of dramatic training can breathe life into your pitches, by bringing the appearance of reality to your characters.

Like an actor, always rehearse your pitch until you feel comfortable with it. Some people rehearse in front of a video camera. This is a great way to see if you are communicating with charm and warmth. Is the tone and emotion of your story communicated with your pitch?

If you don't have access to video gear, merely talk into a tape recorder. Listen and make sure you're not talking in a monotone. Is there spirit and excitement in your pitch? Do you have a clear and engrossing "log line"? Have you broken your story down by the three act structure? What is the character arc of your protagonist? His internal conflict?

Why do we want to root for them? What is your theme? Who is your target audience? Who do you envision as the lead? All of this should be clear on your recording. It's a simple technique, but very effective.

What else can you do as a performer? I've written a comedy that takes place in Ireland. When I pitch the Irish elements, sure an' don't I suddenly shift into a bit of an Irish brogue! It instantly puts a smile on the face of an executive. This has generated excellent interest in the material and I've had many compliments on this pitch.

Actor/playwright Phil Olson writes comedies that take place in Minnesota. He knows the accent, tone and speech patterns of the area. He will always act out the characters with humor. Executives love it! It's just another very simple, but effective, technique.

Actors must learn to *PROJECT*. So must *you*. Don't talk softly! Remember, you can't sell it if they can't hear it.

Further, don't sit there like a bump on a log. You're not part of the furniture. Be *ANIMATED*! Use your hands, gesture a lot, and above all, use facial movements. Unless you're Buster Keaton, deadpan isn't going to work.

Eye contact is crucial. Observing the executive's eyes will let you know when he's bored, when he's engrossed and when something you've said has triggered his interest. By observing the responses of the executive, you can adjust to them. Any good actor will tell you how he hates to do a scene where the other performer doesn't make eye contact. Lack of it creates a lifeless scene. Eye contact creates a vibrant interplay. If you have difficulty with this, practice it until you overcome it. It's a great tool in any kind of communication.

Here's another little known technique from the world of acting. It's what makes an actor appear to be "on." The British are masters at this. Watch any film with Laurence Olivier, John Gielgud, or Alec Guinness.

Even in the quiet moments they are captivating. Why? It's called "stage energy." When a person walks across a stage without purpose, he's a bore. But when he crosses the stage with purpose and energy, he is exciting to watch.

When you first begin to pitch, you'll probably be so full of nervous energy, you won't need stage energy. But, if you get depressed, or feel down, stage energy will give you a vitality that can make you exciting, interesting — someone the executive would want to work with. It is an *ATTITUDE*, how you present yourself. Once you master it, you can turn it on and off, almost like the flip of a switch.

This may seem "airy-fairy," or "far out," but I assure you it is an incredibly useful tool. In my twenties, I wanted to be an actor, but I couldn't stand rejection, so I eventually became a screenwriter. (What a brilliant way to avoid rejection!)

Anyhow, as a student of acting, I learned this technique and I now use it automatically. When I'm with an executive, I'm "on."

Here is the exercise, just as I learned it. (You'll need a little walking space for this.) Begin by standing up and shaking out any stiffness in your arms, neck, and shoulders. Bring yourself up to your full height. Stand as tall as you can without going to your tip-toes. Shift your weight forward so it's balanced on the balls of your feet, rather than your heels. Now close your eyes and imagine a silver cord attached to the top-most point on your head. Imagine that someone is pulling you up by that silver cord.

Begin to take deep breaths in through the nose, out through the mouth. Open your eyes and begin to walk briskly. Feel the exhilaration of marching with your head held high. Think of the excitement of the first game of the season, or a first date, or anything that you look forward to with anticipation. Swing your arms. You will begin to feel the lightness of being and a tingling sensation in your fingers and arms. That's it. You've got it.

Stop! Relax. Let it fall away. Shake it off. Scratch if you have to. Slow your breathing. You're in a low energy mode. Okay? Good.

Now go through the same exercise again. Turn it on, and then deliberately shut it down. You're in control.

Now, can you do it without walking? Can you turn on the feeling merely by self-generation? That excitement you feel is the excitement that the executive will experience in your presence. It will give you the appearance of confidence, enthusiasm, and charisma. Who wouldn't want to work with someone like that?

Use any gimmick, sales technique, or performance technique to captivate the executive, and that will lead to your three-step goal, of getting your script read, sold, and made.

Now you might be thinking, "That's great, Jim, what do I do with the silver cord still attached to the top of my head?"

Overcoming Neurotic Fear
For many people, pitching, performing or even speaking in public can be terrifying. Here is a surprisingly easy cure for this terror.

I learned from a psychologist that the physiological reaction to fear and the physiological reaction to excitement are virtually identical. Therefore, when you are going into a situation that you would normally find fearful, merely psych yourself up by repeatedly thinking, "This is exciting! This is exciting! This is exciting!" But you've really got to throw yourself into the experience of the excitement. This will give you the ability to face your fear, and (eventually) by facing it, you will overcome it.

Overcoming Doubt
We live in a world where there are no certainties. It's only natural to sometimes feel uncertain. We question our own writing ability. This only becomes a major problem when we are stopped by *DOUBT.*

But what is doubt? Is it real? Is it concrete? No, it is something we have self-generated. It exists only in our minds. If this is true, then we can just as easily choose *not* to generate doubt. Simply, will yourself to doubt the doubt, then proceed with confidence.

A panelist at a seminar said some of the best advice she received was: "Don't think! Get out of your own way."

In real estate seminars, it's often said: "Many investors suffer from 'paralysis by analysis.'" With writing, just get it on paper. You can always correct it later. With pitching, go with your best judgment. Doubt the doubt, and proceed with confidence.

There are hundreds of production companies and dozens upon dozens of literary managers and agents. If you screw up with one, it ain't the end of the world. I have found with each failure, with every exposure, I became more courageous.

PITCHING AS SALES
Sales Tricks and Techniques to Captivate a Producer.

Overheard at the Workshop:

"'I've been selling encyclopedias door-to-door for years, so I figured pitching a screenplay to this producer would be easy.' 'Did he buy your script?' 'No, but I sold him a set of encyclopedias!'"

Anything that you are attempting to sell involves verbal, as well as written, communication about the value of the product. That communication is "pitching." With a script, the immediate goal is to get the individual to agree to read your work. Hopefully, that will lead to the ultimate goal of making "the sale."

The key elements in pitching a screenplay and selling a product are the same: *ENTHUSIASM, PASSION* for your project, and *CONFIDENCE.* Convince them you have the best project for them. If *you* question it, they are sure to do so. Remember, "laid back" equals *boring*!

Since pitching and the sale are intertwined, let's look at a few sales techniques and see how they apply to pitching. Here's what some of the Workshop members have said about this.

WORKSHOP MEMBER: "Pitching for me is the same as selling. Pharmaceuticals, communications, computers, insurance policies, I've done them all. Basically, screenplays are the same thing. The number-one thing is to believe in your product and convince yourself that your customer needs it.

"First, you have to find out what his needs are, then get comfortable with the executive. That's called decompression. In the entertainment industry, the people we pitch to are producers and they want their name on the screen. They're fed by ego, as well as by money, but ego is usually the driving force.

"The first thing I do is try to make *them* relax. I talk about anything but me. Talk about them, their company, their prior films. That satisfies their egos.

"At a Pitchmart, realize that they might feel very uncomfortable being there because they're out of their element; they're not in their offices. They can't take phone calls to interrupt you or things like that. They see all these other people waiting in line behind you. Plus, they see the other producers and they think, 'If I turn down this guy, is that one going to take the script?'

"In short, I make sure *they're* comfortable. I smile, 'Hi, how are you?' Then, I make sure I have eye contact. Eventually their look will say: It's time to do business. Now, I've got their attention. Then I'll say, 'Here's what I've got for you.' He'll say, 'Okay, let's hear it.'

"I keep it to two or three minutes. Never talk longer than that. I pause to see if they have any questions and then comes the close, with, 'Would you like to read my script?' You want a yes or a no. If it's no, 'Good, here's my other one.' Two or three minutes, let them ask questions and you're ready to answer them. Then 'Do you want to read it?' Yes or no, that's all you want.

"From selling I have found that when the buyers are inattentive, there are other issues they're concerned with. Personal problems in their private life or perhaps the company they're with is in trouble. I have learned to realize it has nothing to do with my product. It has nothing to do with the script. The number-one thing in selling is eighty percent of the business deals are made whether or not they like the salesperson. So, don't take rejection as something personal. It's purely a matter of their need for the product, in this case the script."

(Note: This eighty-percent figure may well be true in the sales of durable goods, but in the entertainment industry, as discussed earlier, most producers will not work with a writer they don't personally like.)

If executives do say no, realize they're not saying no to your writing, because they haven't read it yet! It's just not the right project for their company, network, or studio. It's just not the right flavor of candy, the right vacuum cleaner or the right Christmas tree that they want to buy at the moment. Don't take it personally! It says nothing about you as an individual, nor anything about your writing ability. It's just not the right fit.

(Note: A key aspect of the above is the importance of "the close." You must finish your pitch with a sales close like, "Would you like to read the script?" Feel free to paraphrase this any way you want, but do not dismiss the importance of requesting a decision on the part of the buyer. "When would be a good time for my attorney [or manager, or agent] to get the script to you?")

Here's another unusual technique. In sales it's called the "take-away." You sit down with an executive, and you say, "I've got two scripts: the first is probably the best thing I've ever written. I've gotten a lot of interest in it, but I'm not quite sure it's for you. The other seems a natural for your company." Which one is the executive more likely to want to hear? Ninety percent of the time, it will be the first one.

You have made it special, by indicating others are interested. He knows he may be able to "take it away" from the buyer. It is similar in principle to the situation where you are stuck with several cases of canned tomatoes, and no buyers. So you label them, "Special, limit one per customer!" and watch them disappear. You have created a perception of scarcity.

By the way, this can work even if you have only one script. Whichever choice he makes, pitch the script you've got.

There's the story of the writer who approached the director/producer John Landis with a project. John loved the concept, and felt Robin Williams would be perfect for the lead. Plus, Robin was represented by the same agent as Mr. Landis. The script had to go through proper channels via the producer, to the actor's agent, to the actor. But the writer bumped into Robin Williams at a charity event and casually asked if he'd had a chance to read his script. Robin said, "I don't recognize the title, tell me about it." My friend didn't want to "step on the toes" of Mr. Landis or his agent, so he said, "No, I can't." With this Robin said, "Well, can you tell me a little something about it?" The writer responded, "No, no, I can't." And it went on. "Well, surely you can...." "No, please don't ask." The more Robin persisted, the more the writer felt he had to refuse.

Robin was totally intrigued by the script before he ever read it. He couldn't wait to get his hands on it! The writer had given Robin Williams the perfect pitch: "I can't tell you about it!" The actor was hooked by the (unintentional) use of the principle of the take-away.

Here's still another technique. I've heard it referred to as "Tone Matching."

WORKSHOP MEMBER: "You have to pick up on the energy of the person you're addressing or pitching to. I have felt a connection when I go with their flow of energy. The more nervous energy they have, the more hyper I get. If they seem calm and a little more cerebral, then I will tone it down and approach the pitch in a more subdued fashion. It all depends on their attitude, energy, or emotional tone level."

The study of neurolinguistics in regard to sales teaches that one of the prime elements is trying to match your energy level to that of the prospective buyer. Neurolinguistics even goes so far as to mimic the body language of the buyer, sitting in the same manner, crossing your legs in the same way, in order to subconsciously bond with the buyer. In theory at least, this makes him feel more comfortable, because you become a reflection of him, and he is therefore more receptive.

The Emotional Tone Scale points out that if you are too far above or below the tone level of the person you are communicating with, your ideas will not be perceived as real. He won't be able to relate.

Again, tone matching may seem far out, but don't dismiss it, because it is a valuable tool in both traditional sales and in pitching. Here are some additional comments by Workshop member Edwin LaRocque, a sales and marketing executive:

"The first time I pitched a screenplay I realized I was selling a product to a buyer. Screenplays are like any other products; they need a buyer — in this case, a producer who has certain market requirements for his company's business plan. The best salespeople have expert product knowledge, and know how it will fit a customer's needs. They also bring enthusiasm and a positive attitude to the meeting. Pitching is very much like that.

"The best salespeople believe strongly in their product. Within 30 seconds, they'll mention its best points, and then listen, ready to answer questions from the buyer.

"And like any presentation, first impressions are important. A recent study says we form an opinion about a person in the first 10 seconds. Interestingly, 80% of what a buyer remembers is the seller's appearance; only 20% has to do with how that product fits his or her needs. In other words, how you look, how you dress, and how you carry yourself are all at least as important as the story you tell!

"A pitch session is no different from a business meeting. Appearance and attitude tell the executive in an instant if this person could be the kind of writer they could work with. We know sex sells. Actually it attracts. Dress to hold their interest, and be prepared to have a great pitch. But wearing anything that would *distract* from the presentation may give the executive an opportunity to say no.

"If you haven't bought a new wardrobe since your high school graduation, and the only clothes you own are the ones you've been wearing for six months while holding your cat in your lap as you type your screenplay, it would be a good idea to freshen things up. Dark or neutral colors seem to be the colors of choice. Anything hot red or road-cone orange-yellow signals caution.

"Piercing may be fashionable but I highly recommend removing your seven ear clasps, the tongue and lip studs, and any nose and eyebrow rings. When you leave, that executive will be talking about you and there's a good bet the conversation will be about your quirky appearance, and *not* your script or your writing ability. Don't distract from the pitch.

"Be well groomed. If you are pitching a romantic comedy, it's best not to show up looking like a skinhead with a goatee, even if you've reformed.

"If you're at a lunch meeting, remember that it's your time to sell, and white bread filling the gaps between your teeth doesn't mean a brighter smile. Avoid soup. Splash spots on a shirt or blouse can be a real distraction. Stay with easy-to-cut and easy-to-eat food.

"Don't bring a 96-ounce iced drink to the executive's desk. It will leave a wet ring big enough to swim in. Don't indulge at the local garlic and wine festival the night before. Those odors will reek through your pores!

"Practice your pitch often. I once got a telemarketing call from a long distance phone carrier. Before I heard his pitch, I said, 'Hey, I'm a screenwriter. Do you go to movies?' The sales rep said, 'Yeah, I go a lot.' 'Great,' I replied, 'because I'd like to pitch you my screenplay in thirty seconds. Do you want to hear it?' 'Sure,' he said, 'go ahead.' And I did.

"'What do you think?,' I asked. 'Would you like to see Mel Gibson in this movie?' He said, 'Man, I wanna see that movie!' I said, 'Thanks' and hung up. That brief exchange gave me a chance to hear a reaction to my pitch.

"Videotape yourself in a mock practice session. Have your 30-second log line ready. View your pitch with a friend and ask for their opinion on your body language and how you told your story.

"Never be late for an appointment. Call the receptionist ahead of time to find out where to park. Double your estimated travel time. Get there 10 minutes early. Chances are you'll be kept waiting, but it's clearly better if you're on time and the executive is late.

"Your enthusiasm and positive attitude will be the first things the executive will notice. A positive attitude begins with making eye contact and having a firm handshake. It's also conveyed by the way you dress and how you sit in the chair across from the executive. Stay on your side of the executive's table or desk. Don't reach over and touch a hand or arm to make a point. People don't like it when you invade their space.

"Even pitching a comedy is serious business. After all, you're asking someone to put up millions of dollars for your story. And that's a business decision. After your first big hit, how you look and what you wear may be less of a factor, but until you receive that first check, dress for success and maintain an upbeat attitude.

"Most sales representatives know they need to make 10 to 20 presentations before they hear 'yes.' A screenplay might require even more persistence. And after an executive says, 'Send me your script; I'll read it,' do what any good salesperson does, keep a follow-up file. In two or three weeks call back.

"Above all, don't put your life on hold waiting for the producer to return your call. Keep that positive attitude and enthusiasm, and most importantly, begin writing your next screenplay."

AN AGENT SPEAKS OUT
Thoughts on Pitching from a Top-tier Agent.

Overheard at the Workshop:

"I thought, since I'm pitching a comedy, I should start off with a joke. So I say to this executive, 'while I was on the freeway driving here, I began to fantasize what it would be like to sideswipe every car. Not hurt anyone. Just knock the phones out of their hands!'

"I start to chuckle. He looks at me like I'm nuts. He says, 'What if they're not speaking on the phone?' I learned my lesson. Never start a pitch with a joke."

For over two decades, Barry Perelman has been a leader in the agency business. He started in the trainee program at the prestigious William Morris Agency, then moved to rival International Creative Management, followed by work for an independent literary agency, before opening the doors of his own firm. He is known as a career-builder, having negotiated the first major deal for such talent as Steven Spielberg.

He has sold and packaged scores of feature films such as *M*A*S*H*, *Babes in Toyland*, *The Amityville Horror*, and *Airbud*, as well as countless TV series like *Columbo*, *The Rockford Files*, *Magnum P. I.*, and *Knots Landing*. He is considered one of the premiere boutique agencies in the industry.

Barry was kind enough to come and talk to our Professional Writers Workshop about writing and the film business in general.

■ ■ ■

KEN: What do you do when you pitch a script to an executive?

BARRY: I'm very well known in the industry, so I use the shorthand of the trade. I'll say something like, "It has the feel of (I pick an appropriate recent box office smash) mixed with the excitement of (another wild hit)." They know I'm not going to send out a piece of garbage, so they usually say, "Send it over." The whole pitch is very short. It has to be. I make over one hundred phone calls a day, so my pitch is rarely more than two or three minutes.

KEN: Do many companies request an outline or synopsis?

BARRY: Of the executives that I talked to, very few actually ask me for a synopsis. The men that I deal with are the VPs of development at the production companies. I give them a one-liner. They ask to see the script. They don't want to read a synopsis. They trust me enough to know the material I send them is professionally done, so they're willing to take a chance, even if they're going to give it to a reader to read.

When I do get that kind of request, it's typically from some executive in a low-budget division. The low-budget guys will ask for a synopsis because they don't have readers available to give them "coverage" like bigger companies do. They want something that they can look at quickly, and if the synopsis turns them on, then they'll take a shot at the script.

(Note: Coverage analyzes a screenplay's strengths and weaknesses and compares it to existing films. It also makes a recommendation as to whether the company should consider buying, producing or casting clients in a particular project. At a glance, executives are able to determine whether the characters, plot, dialogue, and structure are worth the investment.)

With the major companies I deal with today, it's going to depend upon who is making that call. If I make the call, they're going to read the material. They don't want a synopsis. They want their own coverage of the material.

KEN: Are there some subjects that studios don't want to touch?

BARRY: Yes, there are. Even though Oliver Stone made *Platoon*, they're not interested in Vietnam. Negative stories about the religious right are also touchy for studios. They know they'll never get distribution in the southern part of the country.

It's important to be sensitive to how the studios are going to market the picture. There are some things that just don't work for the masses. Look at *Me, Myself and Irene*. If it's funny, you can say anything about sex, but start talking about religion, you're in big trouble.

It's almost impossible to do a black project, because Europeans don't want to see black stars. And right now, 60 percent of the revenue of every film comes from foreign distribution and they all have foreign partners. Those partners don't want to invest in black films. There are exceptions, however, like *Shaft* with Samuel L. Jackson, which was a success.

There is a definite negativity to period pieces. They don't want to make them unless you're of the stature of someone like Michael Mann. He can say, "I want to do *Julius Caesar*" and they'll let him. DreamWorks had the guts to make *Gladiator*, maybe because Spielberg said, "I think it's time." And they went along with it.

Look at the business *Gladiator* has done. Quite frankly, it doesn't have a heavy-duty story line, but it is reminiscent of *Spartacus*. The director Ridley Scott paints pictures better than anybody. He knows what to do with a camera better than anybody. He's brilliant. The way he can shoot a film. The way they did the special effects. Plus, there hadn't been a story about ancient Rome in a long time. It was a gamble and it worked. But, you're talking Spielberg and Ridley Scott, highly acclaimed, veteran filmmakers.

No matter what they say about business expanding, it's actually shrinking. As it expands financially through acquisitions, it becomes narrower at the top, so there are fewer and fewer people who can actually greenlight a picture today.

So studios are running scared. They don't know what to do. They want to make better films, they want good stories. Quite frankly, today studios would rather make a 40-million-dollar picture than an 80-million-dollar picture. They're still going to produce their summer blockbuster films. They may do one for Christmas, and one for summer, which are the big seasons for film. But they're very nervous when it comes to spending millions and millions of dollars.

But, again it's all in the story. If you have an outstanding story, you can attract a production company, and they can attract an actor, and then you've got a picture.

KEN: What do studios mean when they say they want high-concept films?

BARRY: *Gladiator* is a high-concept film because it's an unusual action film. The studios will call something a high-concept film as a way to market the movie. They don't know how to sell films to the public any more. The public's taste is so fickle, they don't know what to give the public.

I can tell you what they don't want. They don't want period pieces unless there's a name attached. Mel Gibson is a different story. He can do *The Patriot*, which is basically a re-do of *Friendly Persuasion* with fight scenes. Did you notice that the fight scenes were almost identical to *Braveheart*? The director's no fool and Mel had a big hand in those fight scenes.

When was the last time there was a War of Independence film like that? The studio took a chance. In the end, *The Patriot* will do well. It may not do well in England, but the French will go because they hate England and they look good in the film. Plus, a key actor in the film is French, which just illustrates how much marketing controls these films.

You have to give a producer reasons to make your film. You have to give them marketing hooks to get a green light. Give them the hooks to attract a star. Otherwise, it's an exercise in futility. There has to be a reason and a way to market your film.

KEN: Should you tell the executive your work is written for a specific star like Mel Gibson or Tom Cruise or....?

BARRY: You shouldn't say that, because it limits you. Instead, I'd say "it's about a forty-ish actor; we're talking about Russell Crowe, Bruce Willis, Mel Gibson, George Clooney, or Harrison Ford." If you can get someone in that group of actors in that age range, then they'll try to get you a deal.

When I say write for a star, I mean make the role so exciting that *any star* will want to do it. Don't limit yourself to one specific star. Don't limit yourself to Mel Gibson. What if Mel Gibson gives it a pass?

You've got to write a screenplay, whether it's for me or someone like me, so the material can be packaged, which means attaching a star, a director, a screenwriter, etc. It's got to be that way, because you need the talent. If Sandra Bullock says she wants to do *Subterfuge*, who is going to say no? Although Sandra has had some failures of late, she's still a big enough female star to get a green light, and this happens to be an action piece, which benefits the project.

By the way, Europeans don't like to see a woman in an action role, because they're still a little chauvinistic. They like their women frozen in time like the early part of the 1900s, not the modern-day American woman. So, when you see a film like *Courage Under Fire* starring Meg Ryan, which is a very well done film, you'd think it would do well. It's brilliantly written and well directed, but it didn't do that well.

I've never been able to get the grosses on how well *Thelma and Louise* did. I can't find anybody who will give me the foreign grosses. I thought it was one of the better road pictures. I loved that film. I just can't get the foreign numbers, so how well could it have done?

KEN: What about stories where the main character is over 60?

BARRY: You hit another negative button. Don't write for that market.

KEN: Why not?

BARRY: They don't go to the movies like teenagers do. That's why the studios say give us edgy, raunchy stories. They're making them for the kids.

The only audience the studios care about is young people, because those kids go out and spend their money on movies, and they certainly don't read the reviews. They're going to go to a film on Saturday night with their girlfriend or boyfriend because that's what they do. That's their entertainment, going out to a movie.

KEN: What about options? Let's say you pitch a story and the producer wants to read your script and then he wants to option it.

BARRY: I hate options. It's a way to legally screw the writer. I never allow my clients to sign one. Just look at it. If a producer options your script, he can flog it all over town. If it doesn't hit, he gives it back to you. What have you got? It's already been shopped to death.

If a legitimate producer is interested, I'll say, "You take it and attach someone. I won't send it out to anyone else." (In an industry this small, my word has to be my bond). "We've done our part with the material, you do your part by attaching talent. And only when the right talent is attached, we'll let you take it to a studio."

But I will work with the guy. I'm known at the major agencies, so I can lead them to the talent. When a studio is interested, then we can talk a deal, based on the budget. Now that makes sense for everyone involved.

But, again, just write a good story. Once you can attract the actor, then you have a picture.

KEN: You talk about attracting stars, but what about *The Blair Witch Project*?

BARRY: Know your market. *Blair Witch* was the needle in the haystack. It was hyped on the Internet first, so kids went to see it. Again, another great date flick.

KEN: They say the Web site was better than the movie.

BARRY: I'm sure it was. They call it a "mockumentary." You can only pull that off once. You can't fool audiences twice. And, believe me, if you didn't have kids, if those were adults, would you have gone to see this film? I don't think so. Big people walking through the forest... Give me a break. It was a phenomenon, a once-in-a-lifetime gimmick that obviously worked.

So, I can't emphasize enough, it's all in the writing. You have control over your own life and what you write. And it's not easy. It's something that requires real effort: the study of film, the study of writing, and knowing what works and what doesn't. But ultimately, good material is the key.

OTHER TIMES TO PITCH
Up for a Job? Up for a Writing Assignment?
The Low-down on How to Nail it.

Overheard at the Workshop:

"I pitched five stories and he hated 'em all. I asked, 'Do you have any advice for me?' He said, 'Yes, get out of the business.' 'But,' I protested, 'I can't get in to get out!'"

In addition to pitching a story for a feature film, MOW (Movie of the Week) or TV show, there are two other kinds of pitches.

One is to *pitch yourself for a job* with a production company, studio, or network.

The second is to *pitch yourself for a writing assignment.*

Pitching Yourself for a Job
Many times new writers will take jobs within the industry to: a) learn all the facets of how a movie or TV show gets made or, b) make contacts that will help in the future, or c) get insight into what scripts get bought and why.

A job on the inside might allow you to sit in on other pitch meetings so that you might learn from other writers what works, or doesn't work, when they pitch.

When you meet an executive who wants to hire someone in a start-up job as an assistant or secretary or in the mail room, the most important advice I can offer you is...*LISTEN*!

Listen carefully to determine what the executive expects of you. What does the job entail? What are the parameters?

You are being hired to fill one of two requirements. Either you will make money for the company or else you will make an executive's job easier. These are the only two reasons you will be hired.

Since you are probably being hired to make your future boss's job easier for him, *let that be your pitch*!

"Here's what I am capable of doing to make your job run more smoothly."

If you have *listened* to what the job entails or what it is the executive needs from you, then in your pitch for the job you can address those needs specifically.

Next, don't be afraid to ask questions about the job or the company.

When I started out, I would ask questions that "subtly" showed off my ambition.

For instance, I might ask: "If the company doesn't start business until ten, is there a way I can get into the office at nine to start getting things in order?"

Cute, huh?

Or, "Would you like me to use a yellow marker to underline any articles about the company before I bring you the morning trades?"

Or, "If you give me a list of annoying people you'd rather not talk to, I won't have to bother you when they call. I'll take down any information for you."

Remember, your pitch should all be about making things easier for the person for whom you're going to be working.

The final part of the pitch is your resume, what you've done and whom they can talk to about your working habits.

Should you tell the executive you want to be a writer some day? Not in the pitch. But, if they ask you what your ultimate goals are, then, by all means, be honest. No executive imagines someone starting out wanting to be in the mail room for the rest of his life!

Finally, if you don't get the job, it means it wouldn't have been a good match between you and the perspective employer anyway, so you're better off.

Instead of moping, start psyching yourself up for the next prospect.

Pitching Yourself for a Writing Assignment

Let's say you've submitted a spec script to a production company, and, while they're not interested in your story, they love your writing. They want to meet you with the possibility of you writing a screenplay based on a story they either own the rights to or have created.

Even though it's their story, you're still going to have to pitch them on hiring you to write it. You might be one of a handful of writers they're interviewing for the job.

First thing, again, is to *LISTEN!* What I usually do, when a company has a project for me to write, is bring a tape recorder. I don't want to forget any of the nuances when they're pitching their story to me.

However, before you turn on the tape recorder, ask permission of the executive. Believe it or not, some execs are queasy about having their conversations recorded.

After you've heard their pitch, they'll almost certainly ask you what you think about their story. Is it something you'd be interested in writing and/or do you have any knowledge of the subject?

After you answer the above questions, they will want to hear what you have to say. For actors, this is called "giving a cold reading." You've just heard the story for the first time and they want to know what ideas you have to enhance their project. Now, it's time. You are about to make "the cold pitch." Remember, your first responsibility is to put them at ease.

Literally what you're saying is, "Give me the ball, let me run with it. Don't worry about a thing. As great as your story is, my screenplay will be even better."

They may ask you for off-the-top-of-your-head ideas. Be careful. Don't get too radical or you might scare them off. Keep your ideas within the structure they have given you. And, don't think for a minute, when the execs meet with other potential writers that they're not throwing out your ideas as if they were their own and asking your rival writers what they think about them.

I have been in meetings where the exec listened to new ideas about his story from the first potential writer, asked the second writer if he thought the new ideas were any good, incorporated the new ideas in his pitch to the third potential writer, and by the fourth was convinced the new ideas were *his own*!

Remember, most executives are not writers and most do not understand the mystique of writing. That's why they're giving their baby to you. *They* don't know what to do with it!

In your pitch, you have to convince them you will handle their baby with care and treat it lovingly.

And finally, whether you're pitching for a job or pitching for a writing assignment: Be prepared, be enthused, be courteous, and be on time. Don't be cocky but be confident. Executives want to see and hear from someone who appears sure of himself. You can't make them feel good about hiring you unless you first feel good about yourself!

A better way would be for the producer to hand out the current version of the script to be rewritten to a number of writers and have them come in individually to pitch the way they would want to do the rewrite.

If the producer does that, do *not* spend any time criticizing or making fun of the first writers. Just go into your pitch, telling the producer how you would make the screenplay better.

Let me tell you about two writers in this situation. One of them came in with six pages of notes and handed out copies to all the executives in the room. He went over all the notes explicitly, one at a time.

The other writer winged it. He came in with no notes. He sometimes stumbled over the names of characters, sometimes forgot significant plot points, and was not really as prepared as the first writer. The second writer knocked himself right out of the competition. The one who had the notes prepared was given the assignment.

Don't you dare try to wing it.

If you have an opportunity to do a rewrite, you're certainly going to have questions, ideas for new scenes, ideas for different plot points or twists in the story that are not presently there. Write them down so you don't forget. That kind of pitch is totally different than when you're pitching your own story. I suggest you not only go in with notes, but feel free to duplicate those notes and hand them out to everybody in the room.

Think in terms of the long run. If someone steals an idea, at least you've made an impression, which will probably pay off in the future.

QUOTES FROM THE TOP
Tips from Executives and Other Writers.

Overheard at the Workshop:

"I pitched my script to a producer, who got very excited. 'That's the best story I ever heard; I can't wait to change it!'"

Pitching well is an asset that will greatly enhance your ability to sell your material. Here is what some of the top industry pros have to say about pitching:

Producer **STEVEN J. CANNELL** has had a series of hit TV shows. His most famous quote on pitching is:

"A good idea told badly sounds like a bad idea."

Cannell explains: "People ask me which I would prefer to do, make a verbal pitch or simply mail in a treatment? When you're in a meeting with a guy, you've got his attention. If I give him twenty-five pages of narrative, he's liable to never read it.

"Something will come up, and it will go on the desk, and something else will come up and something will be put on top of it. But if I've got the guy's attention, I'd better sell him right then while he's looking at me. You can do it if you're a good salesperson.

"When you're presenting something verbally you have to watch your audience very carefully, because when they start to drift, it doesn't matter whether you love what you're saying, you're starting to lose them. If you see their eyes start to go to the window or something like that, just go to the next most interesting thing on your list in your story. Change your tone of voice to wake them up, make them come back to you.

"When I was starting, if my agent was able to get me a meeting with a guy, I'd say 'Make it anytime two weeks from now.' Then I spent two full weeks, eight hours a day, getting ready for a one-hour meeting. And I never missed. I always made a sale.

"When I went in, I'd tell him a fully worked-out three-act structure. I would tell him another idea that was maybe two-thirds worked out. And I'd give him three or four 'what-ifs.' That gave me six or seven items to pitch and one of them was purposely designed to show my ability to structure a story by myself, without help.

"I'd always try to make that idea the most unique I could come up with. I didn't want to hear they'd just bought something similar. If I didn't sell one of my pitched ideas, and that happened only two times, then he would say, 'This is the most prepared anyone has ever been for a story meeting, and out of respect for that, you've got an assignment. We'll work out a story together.'

"If you're out on the street trying to make somebody notice you, you have to be better than anyone else, you really have to be ready to impress him."

LARRY FORRESTER is a former Executive Story Consultant for episodic television. Here's what he says about pitching an idea or a number of ideas for an existing series.

"Unfortunately we've gotten into the habit of judging a man by his performance as a pitcher — as a salesman — rather than for what he puts down on paper."

Forrester continues: "Mistakes are made that way. A very personable man who gets excited and tells the story with a lot of verve is more likely to get an assignment than a shy fellow whose responses are somewhat slower and whose reflexes may not be too sharp. Of course that's no way to judge writing, but pitching is the only game in town.

"There are two meetings I take with new writers. But I will only set up these meetings if I've read a sample of their writing first and have liked what I've read.

"The first get-together is a 'get to know you' meeting. We'll talk. I'll find out about their background, but I won't let them pitch.

"Here's what takes place at the second, official meeting. I will explain to them, 'Look, I don't have any openings on the show at the moment, but it's possible that something that's in the works now will fall down. I will listen to your ideas and I will keep them. If something falls down and your ideas are any good, I'll give them to my Supervising Producer to see if he likes any of them.' I'll listen to the writers' stories, then make notes which simply outline the basic themes of the ideas.

"There's a better chance at the beginning of a new season. In February, the network will give us a commitment for twenty-two one-hour episodes and we'll commit to thirty episodes, to have some in the bank as replacements. That's when I'll say: 'Now, where are those kids I saw last season? Madam secretary, get out my secondary list.'

"Now I'll say to those kids, 'We're renewed, so I want you in here as soon as you can make it with five ideas for this show.' I'll send the newcomer sample scripts and a 'bible' (an outline of all the stories for the coming year) revised for the new season. When the orders from the network come in, that's when the pitching starts — and they'd better have terrific ideas!

"Now if that writer comes in here like Woody Allen and is brilliant and we all love him, or if it's a woman who charms us and pitches a very good, professional original story with verve and emotion, we say, 'Great, go to story outline.' In episodic television, pitching is a critical skill. It is essential to be able to pitch and to respond."

HEIDI WALL is CEO and Executive Producer, Dream City Films.

"Make the pitch short and punchy. To boil down a script to an idea is the essence of good writing as well as pitching. To be honest, you rarely lose by pitching badly. But you always lose by not pitching at all."

Wall explains: "Pitching is trying to turn someone else on to a story that turns you on. You have a passion for the story so you take meetings trying to find another person who wants to play with you at your game. The idea is to connect with another person on an emotional level.

"The most important question to ask yourself is where in your own experience does this story come from? It's that answer that you need to communicate. Why do you love the project? Why *you* care is why *they* will care."

BOB KOSBERG is President of Robert Kosberg Productions, currently at Merv Griffin Entertainment, with over twenty projects in development at various studios around town.

"Visualize your story to the point where it feels as though you're pitching a movie you've already seen. What you're pitching is really the trailer to that movie."

Kosberg comments: "Few people have good ideas. The pitch helps, but the idea is what the executive is listening for. Don't worry so much about how well you speak, but what you're saying.

"If you're not good at pitching, less is more. It's best to do a two-minute pitch than struggle with ten. Don't waste their time. Be polite and be gone. Believe me, they appreciate short and quick, and will gladly invite you back even if they didn't buy the first pitch.

"When an executive hears a good pitch is he thinking about the movie?

Heck, no! He's thinking McDonald's tie-in, theme park rides, and $100-million-dollar box office. A good pitch can be worth a billion dollars."

DAVID MADDEN is a producer/partner in Cort/Madden Productions with a deal at Paramount Studios.

"A writer has to be a lot more that a literary craftsman; he almost has to be a salesman."

Madden's advice: "At major studios like 20th Century-Fox or Warner Bros., it's good to have a treatment to go along with the pitch. This is simply because the executives may want to present the idea to somebody else at the studio and his pitch may not be as strong as the writer's would be.

"The easiest pitches are those for genres that depend largely on plot — horror, thrillers, science fiction, fantasy, and farce to a certain extent. With these, the concept and story line do the work for you; either they're unique and engaging, or they aren't. The genres that depend mostly on characterization and dialogue — romantic comedies, for example — are much harder to pitch.

"Obviously, in your pitch, you want to capture as much of the mood of the movie as possible, especially if an element of suspense is involved. You don't want to give it away beforehand.

"It's got to be told in a way that does not waste time — that doesn't spend a lot of time on exposition and a backstory that isn't really important. It's got to be told with enthusiasm and energy, to suggest that the writer really believes in the story. A lot of it is delivery and personal impression.

"We go so much by instinct that even the initial stage of the talk, before we get to the pitch, almost preconditions an executive to his or her response to the material."

STERLING SILLIPHANT is one of the most successful writers in Hollywood, known best for his work during the "Golden Years of Television."

"You must force yourself to listen, not only to what they are saying, but also to what they are *trying* to say. Very few people are able to sit with a writer and tell him what they really want, otherwise they'd be writing it."

Silliphant suggests: "One of the things I would try to get straight in my head in a story meeting is whether the people that I am meeting with are genuinely able and talented, or assholes. Now, if they are assholes, I would have no advice except that if you need the money, listen. If you don't, leave.

"If they are people you respect — and I would hope that we all have to work for only such people — then I would say don't go into the pitch meeting swearing to get in there and fight like hell for what you've got. That is not the way to go in. The way to go in is to see what the other guy has to say. You will find if you can't live with their suggestions, you have to tell them right then and there, or you have to say, 'I have to go think about it.' But sooner or later you're going to have to bite the bullet on the confrontation with your employer or your producer. Then just hope and pray you can come to a mutual understanding."

LEN HILL, former Vice President, Motion Pictures for TV, for ABC Entertainment, speaking on pitching a Movie of the Week:

"Find the company that you think best understands your style and your ideas, and allow their credibility to be the endorsement for your idea."

Hill's advice: "I would encourage anybody who is thinking of writing movies for television to immerse themselves in what is presently being broadcast. The first requisite of an effective presentation is a familiarity with what the networks have presented in the past, a knowledge of what worked and what hasn't.

"In the pitch itself, you should express the ideas with passion and you should be able to express the concept succinctly. This has been derided for years, the '*TV Guide* mentality.' Yet the reality is that *TV Guide* or similar listing services are the primary way the public is exposed to a program being on the air. If it takes you three paragraphs to tell them what's interesting about the idea, you're not going to sell it to the network, because they don't have three paragraphs to inform the audience of that."

STEVEN KAIRE is an experienced Pitchmeister and seminar speaker to writers around the world.

"The reaction you want from an executive is 'How come no one's ever done that movie before?!' or 'How come I didn't think of that?' "

Kaire suggests: "Go into a meeting confident. Your attitude should be: 'I'm bringing you a gift. If you don't want it, someone else will grab it, and, boy, will you be sorry then!'

"It's not about just delivering a message but having a message worth delivering. What separates people is not pitching skill but writing talent.

"I've never sold an idea to anyone I met for the first time. But by showing I had good ideas, I was always invited back."

STEVE ROSEMARY, Literary Agent, comments:

"One of the most common questions I am asked by producers when they're interested in a new talent is, 'Can I work with this writer?' "

He goes on: "If I couldn't say yes, I wouldn't represent them, because I realized that film, by definition, is a collaborative art. So a young writer who has no track record, who really has no credibility beyond what he's done right there, cannot go in with a chip on his shoulder.

"I find it's crucial that they know when to fight and when not to fight. I'm not saying a writer should not argue with a producer; but there are certain arguments that will bring in a hundred thousand dollars more at the box office and others which will not make any difference. So I say, 'Why fight the little fights?'

"This is very hard for new writers because they have never had their work judged and they are sensitive to it.

"The writer has to be willing to immediately forego any type of ego involvement in the script."

SCOTT ROSENBERG, author of *Con Air*, *Armageddon*, *Gone in 60 Seconds*, and many others, says:

"Always cast your pitches."

Rosenberg elaborates: "Sometimes in a pitch, I realize the concept has gone right over the head of the executive, so I'll casually mention, 'and of course, I envision Mel Gibson and Julia Roberts playing the leads.' Suddenly, the vision becomes crystal clear, and a lost pitch becomes a sale.

"Naturally, you'll want to do some research to pick names within the budget range of the producer and try to avoid choosing his bitter ex-wife. Other than that, it works like a charm."

JENNIFER LERCH, author of *500 Ways to Beat the Hollywood Script Reader*.

"It's a pitch-driven business."

She explains: "Can you sell it in one or two sentences? You want a concept that you can sum up in one quick line that leaves the person who reads or hears that line wanting more."

THE PITCH BEFORE THE PITCH
Getting the Meeting with a Query Letter.

Overheard at the Workshop:

"I have this meeting with a very important producer and I don't want to mess up. And even though I've been taught not to, I memorize my pitch. I've got it down pat, every word, every phrase, every intonation. I go to his office and pitch it perfectly. I don't miss a beat.

"I see he's excited. He jumps up, goes to the door and yells out, 'Tina, Marlene, Gary, get in here!' They take seats and he says to me, 'These are my associates. Let's hear the pitch again.'

"So I repeat it. I don't change a thing, not a word, a phrase, an intonation. When I'm done he says, 'I liked it better the first time.'

"I waited until I got outside the building before I screamed."

All projects require either an agent, a manager or an entertainment attorney to represent the writer. So eventually, you'll have to have representation. If you've pitched your script to an executive who wants either to option it or buy it outright, any literary agent, manager, or attorney will be glad to represent you because you've already got a deal. They can earn an instant commission.

Another way is to send query letters seeking representation. There are four methods I suggest for contacting a "Rep." The first is to contact the Writers Guild of America and ask them to send you a list of all the agents. These are all licensed and signatory literary agents (you don't want any other kind) who represent script writers and screenplays.

The Writers Guild list is all-inclusive and updated constantly. Next to many of the names of the agencies, there will be either one or two asterisks. The single asterisk means that they will read a screenplay unsolicited from any writer who sends one in. The double asterisk next to some of the agency names means they will only read scripts from new writers if the writer mentions a name that is known to the agency. If you've taken the time to buy this book, you may use my name. Say, "Ken Rotcop suggested I contact you about my new script. I'm looking for representation."

Now, half the agencies that have the double asterisk know me, half of them don't. The ones that don't know me, will simply say, "We don't know who Rotcop is" and that will be the end of that.

Of the half that know me, half of them like me and half of them don't. Of the half that like me, they will say, "Ken Rotcop? Fine, send the script." The half that don't will say, "We wouldn't read a script from a Rotcop writer if it was the last script on Earth." If my math is right, one fourth of the literary agencies who have the double asterisk will read your script if you mention my name!

Second is the Hollywood Creative Directory's *Agents and Managers Directory*. It would behoove you to buy a copy of this book, which is updated three times a year. It is very important because it lists all the agents within the agencies. When you call an agency, ask them for a specific agent. Because now you have their name.

You will either get the agent on the phone or you will get the secretary, his assistant, or a junior agent. These are people you can talk to. Their job is to screen all calls and protect their bosses from the likes of you. But these secretaries or junior agents are always looking to score points with their bosses. So if you tell *them* about your script, *they* will likely ask to read it, knowing that if they can recommend your screenplay to their boss and the boss likes it, they can move up the ladder of success! And so will you!

Third, if you don't get a copy of the Hollywood Creative Directory, call an agency and ask the receptionist who answers the phone which agent handles new writers. That's another way to get the names of agents and then ask to speak to that agent. Make sure you write down the name and ask for the correct spelling so you won't forget it. Again, you'll get either his assistant, the secretary, or a junior agent who works under him. See if you can convince them to read your script.

Now, if you feel uncomfortable making cold calls, you can send a query letter. But send it to a *specific agent*, not just to the agency. Again, get those names using the abovementioned methods. Send that query letter to every agency that has an asterisk, asking them if they will read your screenplay.

Fourth, from time to time an ad will appear in the trade papers, such as *Daily Variety* asking for scripts. These are usually small independent companies that are looking for lightning in a bottle. They're hoping to find the screenplay that either they can produce themselves with some financing, or that they can turn over to a bigger production company or studio after making a deal with you. That way, they latch themselves onto your script with the hope that they will get a producer's credit if the script gets produced.

I tell the writers in my workshop to be extremely cautious in sending scripts out in response to ads in the trade papers. You have no idea who these people are. What I would do first is send them a query letter and ask for their qualifications. Give them your phone number, so they can call you back. Then, if you're happy with the response you get, if you feel comfortable with who they claim they are and what they plan to do with your script, then and only then would I send them a screenplay.

Again, when you're a first-time writer, you really do want to get as much exposure as possible, so I'm not saying you shouldn't send your scripts to these people, but I'm saying check them out first.

When you send the script, include a cover letter and keep a copy so that you have a paper trail. Most new writers are paranoid about exposing their material to someone they do not know. But you have to take risks in this business, because you never know where the deal is going to come from! However, you must protect yourself whenever possible. Always make copies of cover letters.

Here's a good idea: with your query letter, enclose a self-addressed, stamped postcard. On the postcard neatly print the following questions for the producer to answer:

Please check the appropriate box and return to me.

☐ Send me your script immediately.

☐ My plate is full. Sorry.

☐ Too busy right now. Call me in three weeks.

Thank you,

_____

(Name/title)

Writers in my workshop say the response is nearly 100 percent!

Of course, on the opposite side of the card put a postage stamp with your name and address as the receiver. Be sure to put the name and address of each producer as the sender or you'll get a bunch of responses and you won't know who they came from!

Don'ts for Contacting Agents
In your query letter don't get cute with lines like, "I'm going to put your agency on the map with this one." Or, "They'll be lining up to buy this script from you."

Also don't pepper the pitch with lines like, "This story will have you on the edge of your seat." Or, "This hysterical, zany comedy will have you laughing an hour after you've read it." Or, "It packs a wallop," or "It's fast and furious, with non-stop action." Those are all wonderful catch-phrases for the poster when the movie gets made, but you don't want to use them in your query letter. You just want to tell them enough to entice them to want to read your script.

What a Letter Should Have

First, make sure you have your name, address and phone number at the top. Second, the title and genre of the script. Example: I am seeking representation for my screenplay, *Shanghai Noon*, a western/martial arts comedy.

Third, include a brief pitch telling about the main characters, the conflict and the action. Here's how I would pitch *Shanghai Noon*.

When the Princess is kidnapped from the forbidden city and taken to America, the Emperor sends four of his trusted guardsmen to get her back. Actually, three of his trusted guards and one goof-ball. Three get shanghaied. Guess which one gets away and single-handedly has to save the Princess from the dastardly evil villain and his scurrilous henchmen?

Arriving in the Old West, he picks up an American sidekick, a cowboy who is totally inadequate at fighting but talks a good game. Even more inadequate, of course, is our hero the Asian whose martial arts can best be described as bizarre. Yet together they must save the Princess, do in the bad guys, fall in love with different women and try not to leave the Old West in shambles. They succeed in three out of four.

Again, this is not a synopsis of the entire story. It's just enough to hopefully entice them and give them a sense of the adventure and its comedic possibilities. It also gives them a sense of your writing ability.

For instance, "I've always been interested in mixing three cultures in the 1890s, Indians, the Chinese, and cowboys, and then having them caught in the crucible of the Early West. It intrigued me and I have never before seen this combination in a movie."

Fourth, make it short and to the point. "May I send you my screenplay for your consideration?" Can be shortened to "May I send you my screenplay?" And "I know you are busy, so I really appreciate you taking the time to respond, and please know I appreciate any and all considerations, and I look forward to hearing from you" can be shortened to "Thank you" and your name.

Three questions I can hear you asking:

1.   How soon can I follow up with a phone call if I don't get a response? Generally, wait four days, then send the script. After that, wait three weeks, then call asking if they've read your script yet.

2.   Can I send out more than one query letter at a time? Yes, I would send out dozens; do not wait for an individual response. Flood the market.

3.   Should I list my experiences? If you read the chapter on resumes, only include activities or experiences that reflect your knowledge of the material you're writing about.

Someone once said, don't be dull or desperate in your pitch letter. To that I would add, and make sure you tell them something they ain't heard or seen before.

Something to Remember
If in doubt about what to include in your story synopsis, include the big event, the crises and the showdown.

Do not go on and on about seeking representation. In other words, "while we have never met, and while I did get your name in the Hollywood Directory, I know your agency represents many important writers and has a lot of juice in the industry, and therefore I hope you like my script and take me on as a client." You don't have to belabor the point about needing representation. They know, that's why you've written them. Don't butter up the agents.

Do not send a treatment, synopsis, or a script with the query letter. Wait until they respond, then send your script.

Remember, a pitch, be it in person or in a query letter, is not a synopsis of the entire story. Just enough to entice them, and also give them a sense of it. A sample of a query letter is in our next chapter, DIFFERENT FORMS OF PITCHING.

DIFFERENT FORMS OF PITCHING
The Difference Between a Synopsis, Treatment, Log Line, Phone Pitch, and Query Letter.

Overheard at the Workshop:

"He said he loved me, loved my story and loved my writing — then I never heard from him again."

You will occasionally hear of projects being sold based only on the pitch. In this case, the producer has bought an idea for a screenplay that is yet to be written. That is almost never done except with an author whose prior screenplays have been made into films that did well at the box office. No producer will take such a risk with someone who doesn't have an incredible track record.

That's why, the first-time writer *must* write a complete screenplay so if the producer likes the pitch, the writer can immediately follow up with the screenplay.

Remember that you are pitching both the story and the marketability of the future script. Three things are key to this kind of pitch.

The first aspect of your pitch is the question: "What is it about my story that will have big stars drooling to be in it?"

The second aspect is your impression of what the poster will look like. How do you grab your target audience?

Finally, you must convey six or seven visual highlights that will create an exciting trailer. These are called "the money shots" — the scenes that sell the movie.

Basically, there are five ways in which to communicate the essence of your story to an executive. Here are the differences between a face-to-face pitch, a log line, a synopsis, a treatment, and a phone pitch.

I have chosen to use for example, *The Unsinkable Molly Brown*, a movie that a lot of people have seen.

The "Log Line" is the very short, *TV Guide* version of the story. It must hook the reader's interest in just a few lines. Who's the protagonist? What's the essence of the story?

This is a crucial element, so every writer must have a concise, captivating log line for each of his scripts. Many writers memorize their log line(s), so they can snap it out at an instant's notice.

Many pitches begin with the log line. Then if there is even a modicum of interest, proceed to your full pitch.

But this can be tricky. Let's, for instance, try to figure out the log line for *The Unsinkable Molly Brown*.

One log line could be:
An ambitious backwoods woman marries a wealthy man but can't find acceptance in Denver's high society.

Another possible log line might be:
An ambitious backwoods woman travels to Europe to learn culture and charm but in so doing drives her husband away.

Both are interesting possibilities as a log line. Here's a third possibility: Inspired by a true story, an indefatigable woman returns from Europe on the Titanic in hopes of winning back her husband.

Which is the best log line?

The first one is best for an older audience. Young people couldn't care less about high society.

The second log line sounds like a perfect pitch for the Family Channel or any of the cable channels that cater to a female crowd.

The third has two buzz words that will make a potential audience sit up and take notice. Anytime a network can claim their movie is "based on" or "inspired by" a true story, their ratings go up at least five points. So "inspired by" is buzz word number one.

The second buzz word is "Titanic". First, because audiences can't seem to get enough about stories involving that ill-fated ship, and secondly, because it's familiar, so audiences can immediately identify with it.

However, talking about "ill-fated," there is one word in the third log line that will turn people off and keep many from watching the show. The word is "indefatigable." Too long, too many syllables, and the word may be unrecognizable to a great many. If a word causes confusion or makes one stop to think, don't use it. Six syllables is, unfortunately, about three syllables too many for the average audience.

In summary, the first log line would attract a more mature audience, the second would grab the women, and the third would be for a more general audience. Again, always think marketing.

A *synopsis* is a condensation of a story that touches on all the major characters. For a writer, a synopsis is a sales tool. It must be engaging and it's usually written in the style or tone of the script. A comedy should make you laugh, a thriller should have the reader on the edge of his or her seat, etc. Of course, brevity is essential.

SYNOPSIS: *The Unsinkable Molly Brown*

Shoeless, dirty and spunky, Molly Tobin is the only daughter of a penniless Irish immigrant in Hannibal, Missouri, but she dreams of golden things. Stuck in these dreams, she marries lucky prospector Johnny Leadville Brown who strikes it rich so that her dreams seem closer than ever.

But uneducated and untrained, Molly Brown can't find acceptance in the society circles of wealthy Denver. Her tireless hunt for acceptance leads her to the casinos of Monte Carlo where she wins popularity but loses Johnny. He takes off for home, leaving Molly to the attentions of a slick nobleman. Realizing that it's Johnny she wants after all, she sails after him on the doomed Titanic. But it takes more than an iceberg to keep Molly away, once she's made up her mind.

Arriving back at their cabin in the Colorado mountains, Molly convinces Johnny it's him she wants more than wealth, nobility, or acceptance by snooty Denver society.

That's a good synopsis of this story.

As mentioned, the synopsis touches on all the major characters and all the major plot points. A pitch doesn't do that. In a pitch, you put all the emphasis on the protagonist whose story it is, and you tell the pitch from her or his point of view. What makes that character unique, and somebody we should care about?

Or, if it's an action-adventure movie, you might want to tell it from the villain's point of view, because he's the one who puts the story in motion.

Heroes only get involved in stories in one of two ways. One way is through curiosity. Somebody comes to them and arouses their interest, or they see something that intrigues them, and out of curiosity, they find themselves getting involved in a situation.

Indiana Jones stories always had Indiana getting involved out of curiosity. The man was a scientist, an archeologist, and there was always somebody coming to him and telling him of a wondrous discovery that could be his if he would take a certain assignment. Out of professional curiosity, Indiana would get involved.

The other way a hero gets involved is where he innocently gets sucked into the story, causing him to react. Somebody causes action, the protagonist responds, and that drags him into the story.

A typical Alfred Hitchcock film had Jimmy Stewart on vacation. He witnesses a crime. He reports what he's seen to the police and immediately becomes their prime suspect. The actual killer hunts down Stewart because he knows Stewart can finger him.

The innocent tourist on vacation is suddenly in a cat and mouse game with the police *and* the killer.

Those are the only two ways that I know of where a protagonist gets involved in a story, out of curiosity or as a reaction to stimuli. You may think, "What about somebody who's driven to find a goal?" But that goal is the (hopefully logical) response to external stimuli (the villain's actions) or a response to curiosity.

The villain or antagonist is the one who causes the action. He always has an agenda. He always has a reason for wanting to act upon the protagonist. He's infinitely more interesting, particularly at the beginning of the story, because the antagonist wants something desperately, be it money, power, or possessions. Antagonists tend to be more colorful, more interesting, because they're always a little off-center, crazed by something; so another way to pitch stories would be from the antagonist's point of view rather than the protagonist.

In any of the James Bond movies, it's always the Dr. Nos of the world, the Goldfingers of the world, who not only get the title of the film, but are infinitely more interesting than James Bond himself, who really is a relatively one-dimensional character. Sure, when he goes into action he's marvelous, but other than that, he's a sophisticate, who never really looks for trouble. Trouble comes to him. Trouble finds him and he must then react to the troubles.

THE PITCH: *The Unsinkable Molly Brown*

> A teenage girl is a hillbilly. She's uneducated, she never wore shoes in her life, she's been brought up to roughhouse with her three older brothers. But she has a dream to get out of the cabin she lives in so she can become rich, sophisticated, and famous. Lo and behold, she does.
>
> But, while she is rich, she won't be happy until she is accepted by Denver's high society, who call themselves Denver's 32. The thirty-two wealthiest families in town.
>
> No matter what she does, the parties she holds, the fancy outfits she buys, the butlers she hires, Denver's 32 will not accept her. She's gruff, she's uncouth, and she's unsophisticated. So no matter how much money she has, she's shunned by high society. But this hillbilly vows vengeance. Would you like to read the story?

Notice I didn't mention the Titanic. I didn't mention the husband or the romantic nobleman. I gave the producer "a taste" of what the story is about. The protagonist is our hillbilly. The antagonist, in this case, is not a single person but a group of people, the "Denver 32." In my pitch, I tell them that the protagonist wants "to be accepted" and what the antagonist does to stop the protagonist — i.e., they reject her.

Hopefully, this pitch will be enough to entice the producer to ask questions about the story. The sweetest words a writer can hear when pitching is "What happens next?"

Now you're not pitching, you're telling. The pressure is off, you've got 'em hooked.

Now, dear reader, it's up to you to reel him in.

"How'd she get rich?" You can then bring in the husband.

"How'd she get revenge?" Talk about Europe, the sleazy nobleman, the husband splitting.

"What happens next?" Here you tell them about the Titanic, her snubbing the "Denver 32," her winning back her hubby, and the lesson she learns: "Money don't buy you happiness, only love does."

At that point, your part of the pitch is done and now it's up to the producer to decide whether he chooses to read your screenplay or pass. Remember a pass is not a personal rejection, it just means your story is not necessarily *his* kind of story.

The reason I chose *Molly Brown* is because you don't have a fixed antagonist. You simply have a woman who has a desire for fame and fortune and the antagonist is a society who likes to pigeonhole people, a group who decides who's in and who's not.

Molly Brown would not be an easy piece to pitch from the villain's point of view. Ask yourself, who is the most interesting character? Who is the most colorful character? If it's the protagonist, then the pitch should be from the protagonist's point of view. If it's the antagonist, which it is in many situations, then the pitch could be told from the antagonist's point of view.

Remember in your pitch to mention what the conflict of the story is. In my research, I have found there are five conflicts.

Man Versus Man	(Easy, Hero must stop villain)
Man Versus the Establishment	(Hero takes on high society, big business, or the government)
Man Versus the Machine	(Hero takes on flying saucers, robots, or runaway computers)
Man Versus Nature	(Hero must climb a mountain, defeat a bear in the wild, or capture and tame a whale)
Conflict of the Soul	(Hero must decide between the one he loves and a chance for fame and fortune)

There are two other pitches that I want to discuss. One is the *phone pitch* where you're trying to get an agent or a production company to take a meeting with you and they ask you on the phone what your story is about. That way, if they hate the pitch over the phone, or they have something similar in the works, or they know a movie like it is already being made, they will discourage you from coming in. On the other hand, if you've piqued their interest over the phone, they will feel it worth setting up a meeting.

The phone pitch is one time where I think it's a good idea to first write down what it is you want to say, because they're not going to see you reading something. This assures you of getting down all of your salient points. If you forget something in a pitch meeting, you'll have time to say, "Oh, wait a minute, I forgot an important point" and you can bring it up.

On the phone, pitches are usually very quick, so you don't want to hang up and say, "Oh my goodness, I forgot a very important part." When it comes to the phone pitch, write it down before you pick up that phone.

And keep it short. Shorter than a pitch meeting. You have, maybe, four sentences to sell the person on the other end of the line.

Back to *The Unsinkable Molly Brown*, if I had written the script and I were going to pitch it over the phone, and an executive on the other end said to me, "Tell me in a couple of lines what your story is about," that's when I'd start with the log line, then embellish it with a few more cogent story points. This gives the executive a feeling of what the project is about. In the shorthand of the business, the log line is sometimes called a "thumbnail." It's called that because your thumbnail would cover the two or three lines describing your story in the *TV Guide*.

Another word they use is "shorthand," which means "tell me the genre by giving me similar titles of movies already made." For instance, I was recently hired to write a screenplay and the producer said, "The shorthand is *My Life As a Dog* meets *Summer of '42*." I immediately knew he wanted a movie about hormones overtaking a group of kids, while our protagonist is going to be smitten by an "older woman."

Other shorthand ideas I've heard pitched are: A black *Dances with Wolves* or *Animal House* meets *Coyote Ugly*.

Incidentally, if you're going to use shorthand, make sure you refer to movies that were big financial hits!

The final pitch is the "letter pitch" or "query letter." This is where you're writing for representation to an agent or a manager, and you say that you have a script you think they would be interested in representing. You give them a couple of lines to intrigue them.

The pitch in the letter or the pitch on the phone are very similar insofar as they should only be a couple of lines, just enough to pique their interest. Those are the only two cases where writing your pitch down is appropriate.

I don't believe in writing down and reading your pitch when you're meeting face to face. I even have problems with writers who memorize their pitch before the pitch is made. It loses the spontaneity of being conversational. Another danger: When you're verbally pitching and you're sitting there with your eyes down on a piece of paper, you're not eye-balling the executive. And in reading your pitch, there's no excite-ment, no passion.

So what should this letter look like? Here's a sample. (I'll use the *Molly Brown* story for the last time, I promise.)

> Zane Crisp
> c/o The Zane Crisp Literary Agency
> 4171 Stardust Lane
> Hollywood, CA 90028

> Dear Mr. Crisp:
> I have just finished a screenplay titled *The Unsinkable Molly Brown* and am looking for representation.
> My story, a dramedy,[1] follows a teenage girl — a hillbilly, a poor white trash type — who, with her husband, tries to join Denver's high society. Because they are gruff and unsophisticated they are blacklisted, so they head off to Europe to acquire sophistication.
> Our heroine, Molly, wins over the heart of a Count who loves her down-to-earthiness. But she loses her neglected husband.
> Surviving the Titanic disaster, she becomes famous, sticks *her* nose up at Denver's society, and heads for the backwoods to win back her loving husband.
> I will send you my screenplay in a few days for your consideration.
> Should you wish to talk to me sooner, I'm at (818) 555-5555.

> Thank you,

> [Your name here.]

Never write, "If you would like to read my screenplay I can be reached at...." That requires the agent to call you to get the script, and he just might not get around to it.

---

[1] A dramedy is part drama, part comedy — and yes, I know *The Unsinkable Molly Brown* was a musical, but forget the music for our illustration.

You must take the initiative and *send* your screenplay. He may read it, he may send it back, or he may junk it.

But a one-out-of-three chance of getting your script read is better than no chance at all. And by including your phone number, you've given him the option to call should he not like your pitch at all, and not want you to send the script.

Otherwise, wait about four days from the time you've sent the pitch letter, and then follow it up with a copy of your script.

The *phone conversation*. If you're lucky enough to get through to an executive at a production company or a studio, and you want to set up a meeting, say "I'd like to come in and meet with you and talk to you about the screenplay I've just finished."

They might say, "Can you give me the thumbnail on it?" or "Can you give me the log line or the shorthand?" Whatever phrase they use, be prepared. Have all your bases covered. By having three sets of answers already written down in front of you, you should be able to entice the executive to set up a meeting with you.

I must say it's very, very difficult if you are an emerging writer and do not have representation to have a production executive take a meeting with you or even have you send in the script. They almost always insist upon representation. There are some companies that will have you send them the script if it's not represented, but only after you've signed a release form.

My advice is sign the release forms even though they state that the company can use material "similar to yours" and that you will have no retribution. In truth, those release forms are not legally binding, since the writer signs them under duress. If you are forced to do something against your will in order to make a potential sale, you are acting "under duress." Since they won't read your script unless you agree to sign their release form, and therefore, are preventing you from selling your screenplay, that becomes "duress." Therefore, I wouldn't worry about signing it.

Include a cover letter with your screenplay title, the date, and any pertinent information. Of course, keep copies of all correspondence! That way you have maintained a paper trail. The main thing is to get that script into the hands of somebody who can do something for you, even if it looks like you're signing your life away (or at least your screenplay).

(Note: I am not an attorney and can't give legal advice, but I believe your attorney will agree with the above.)

Originally, a *treatment* was usually based on a novel, a biography, a short story, or a newspaper or magazine article that a company had optioned. Then, it would be turned over to a writer whose job it was to translate how he would turn the material into a screenplay. In other words, a treatment meant taking the material in its original form and "treating" it so the executive could see how the movie version would look.

Now however, there is a tendency in the movie industry to interchange the words *synopsis*, *treatment*, and *outline*. When you're asked to write one or the other, be sure you and the producer are "on the same page" and have a clear understanding of what he expects.

PROTECTING YOUR WORK
Copyright, WGA Registration, and Self-registration.

Overheard at the Workshop:

"The house was on fire! Through burning timbers, I rushed into the den to save my computer. It had all my scripts, all my practice pitches, all my ideas for futures stories! I grabbed it and rushed out of the flame-licked, smoke-filled house. The computer was safe! Then I went back in for the baby."

Let's assume that you are an emerging writer. Now let's assume that you've come up with a wonderful *idea* for a screenplay, and per chance you meet an executive who is looking for material.

The question arises, should you pitch your idea to the executive, on the chance that if he likes it he'll hire you to write the script? The answer is: *forget it*! He's not going to hire an untried writer. If you do not have any credits, and if you do not have any screenplays that you've written to give him as examples of your work, the chances of him hiring you — that is, actually paying you for your idea — is next to nothing. No executive will want to spend money and take a risk on a wannabe.

You're much better off asking that executive if you might some day contact him, because you're working on a project and you'd like very much for him to read it when it's ready. Nine out of ten executives will say, "Absolutely."

Don't give him any details, even if he asks, because ideas are floating all over Hollywood and ideas are *not* copyrightable. He just might walk away with it, even though he might do it without maliciousness.

Rod Serling, when he was producing *The Twilight Zone*, kept a "war chest" (his term) containing many, many thousands of dollars, because

89

he was constantly being besieged by people who said, "Hey, Rod, I saw your show last week and that was the story I gave you at that party we attended eight months ago," or two years ago, or five years ago. Or, "I ran into you in the supermarket and I gave you that idea. You used it and I expect to be paid for it."

Well, rather than fight them, Rod would have somebody in his company go to the war chest and send a check, along with a note saying, "Thank you for the idea." He let it go at that. Why? Because Rod said he *didn't know* where he came up with the ideas. He was constantly being bombarded by people on the outside who were throwing concepts at him, pitching projects to him. He said he could very well have gotten it from somebody. Therefore, he said he'd rather give them some money to placate them, than argue with them, fight them, or end up in a lawsuit.

Before you go off to pitch your script, make sure it's registered. There are three ways I know of to register material. One is through the Writers Guild of America. They charge $20 to register your screenplay, and that $20 holds the script for five years. You can renew the registration every five years. Registering your script provides proof of when you actually finished your screenplay.

In other words, if a company claims they had a similar script, but they saw yours before the registration date on theirs, there is a good chance they stole material from you and they'd be setting themselves up for a lawsuit. (A fairly common occurrence in Hollywood.)

The second way is the "poor man's copyright": send your screenplay in an envelope to yourself. And *never* unseal that envelope, so that the date stamped on the envelope will hold up in court as the date that your script was finished. If you choose this method, always write on the outside of the envelope what's on the inside. Also, always mark it, "To be opened by a JUDGE only!" When you take it to the post office, it's best to have them turn it over, and put the date stamp (the cancellation stamp) in all four corners. So then there's no question that it's never been opened. If it's just stamped on the front, it's not as secure. It could be steamed open, for example.

The third way is to send your script to the Library of Congress in Washington, DC and have them copyright the script. That costs $30, and that's for your lifetime plus seventy years. Should there ever be a problem, you can use the attorneys from the Library of Congress to represent you in any court case.

Remember, it is imperative to protect yourself so that if anybody ever steals your material — and yes, it does happen — the canceled stamp, or the return card from WGA, or the Library of Congress will be proof of when your script was finished. This paper trail is essential if you accuse someone of stealing your material. With it, you have a very good lawsuit, and an excellent chance of collecting.

THE PITCH QUEEN
From Selling Flowers to Screenplays. Boy, Can She Pitch!

Overheard at the Workshop:

"So I did my pitch and he said, 'You pitched me the same story last year.' 'How'd you remember?', I replied. 'How could I forget it? It's haunting. It's been etched in my mind since the last time I saw you.' I said, 'Wanna buy it?' He says, 'No, it's not my cup of tea.'"

The information in this chapter was contributed by Maria James, who went from peddling flowers two years ago to selling screenplays today. She's had two movies produced and currently has two films in development. Boy, can she pitch!

"Everything I know about pitching I learned from Ken and from watching *The Player*, one of my favorite movies. (Is that a character flaw?) My fellow writers dubbed me the Pitch Queen because, if there's a room full of producers, I'll get more reads than anyone else. ('A read' is defined as a producer asking to read one of my scripts.) They say it's because I wear tight dresses and high heels, but they're *WRONG*. I don't — well, I usually don't — wear tight dresses, and I can't even walk in high heels.

"What I can do is talk. I can talk to a chair. It doesn't have to have anyone sitting in it. That's my big secret. I'm enthusiastic, especially about my own work. It doesn't mean I'm always confident, but I always appear confident and excited, and absolutely positive that if you read my script, you'll have a winner. (Lots of coffee helps here, too.)

"So if you ask me what the most important thing a writer needs to have in order to pitch a script, it is the ability to sell. Basic salesmanship. Look them in the eye, engage them in chit-chat. Don't over- or undersell.

Don't give them too much information. Believe in your product and be proud of it. There are books on selling. I've read one or two and I recommend it. And no matter how bad you bomb out, you can always save the day with a bright smile and a big dose of exuberance. I've messed up pitches in the most awful way, seen that completely lost look in the producer's eye and said, 'You know, that was a terrible pitch, but the script is really great and you should read it!'

"What do I do? The first thing after the smile and exchange of 'How ya doings' is to hand the producer my resume and my business card. I then shut up. I give him a chance to look over my resume, which is not terribly impressive, but it's better than nothing. I know whether or not they've looked at my card because they generally laugh when they read it.

Maria James

Writer

818.555.1212

Paris   London   San Francisco   Glendale

(You see, Glendale is this little suburb of Los Angeles...well, *I* think it's funny.)

"Somewhere I read: *In sales he who talks first, loses* — so I let the producer talk first. I wait until he's done messing with his papers, writing notes, and then I get eye contact. Just sitting there, watching him read my resume and look at my card, I get a moment to get my act together and size him up. Sometimes that's when I decide what I'm going to pitch.

"When I have more than one script to pitch, the one I pitch is always my personal favorite. Or at least that's what I *say*. I usually pitch 'chick flicks' to women, blockbusters to big studio wannabes, quirky films to the artsy types. But strangely, my most sensitive chick flick went over great with this young guy on the Universal lot, so go figure. Whatever art there is in deciding what-to-pitch-where, I haven't mastered it yet.

"When I can't figure it out, I'll ask, 'Would you do a period piece? How about a teen comedy? Superhero flick? Do you like romantic comedies?' Hopefully, I get some sort of clue. Occasionally, they'll tell you exactly what they are looking for, and you could get lucky and have that script.

"Once I start, I try to get the producer engaged, get him to say something, even if it's just to agree or disagree. I'll say, 'Did you like being a teenager?' It doesn't matter what he or she says, I'm going to pitch the script on teenagers. They may say, 'Not really' or 'It was okay' or 'I loved it.' Whatever they say, my response is: 'I hated it; it was the worst time of my life. This is the story of Michelle, the most miserable of miserable teenagers....' And I proceed to pitch. This accomplishes several things. I've gotten them to say something to me, maybe something personal, at least started a conversation. I've also shown them that I'm writing about something I know about. If you read books about writing, they're always pushing the write-from-the-heart line.

"Another opening, 'Ever been divorced?' (Quite often I get a 'yes' to this. What a surprise in this town!) 'Ever wished your ex was dead?' Again, it doesn't matter if you get the nod or not, they know what you're talking about. 'This is my what-I-want-to-do-to-my-ex story. You've got this woman whose husband beats her. She wishes he were dead and then she gets her wish.' (If you do use this approach, you might have to do some serious listening before you start your pitch.) But that can work, too. Once you've heard their deep dark secrets, they start to think you're a friend, and they might just read your script out of loyalty.

"Another question I've opened with is 'Do you know where the first American gold rush was?' (Producers always give the wrong answer;

nobody knows this.) 'No, it was in Georgia in 1832 when they discovered gold on Cherokee land. Now the Cherokees weren't savages. They had their own alphabet, their own newspaper, and they were trying hard to learn American ways. My story takes place....'

"Another great way to go is to tell a story about my life that explains how I got the idea for the script. 'I used to have this boyfriend and we had the strangest relationship. He was younger than me, very handsome, worked with his hands, and he couldn't talk at all about his feelings. And as you can tell, *I* can talk to *fruit* at the grocery store and sometimes it answers. Anyway, I went to Ken — my writing teacher — and I told him that I wanted to write a love story about the two of us and he gave me this angle. So this is the story of....'

"This is my best one: 'I got the idea for this script because I have a pair of Batman sunglasses. Whenever I wore them to my son's daycare, all the kids would surround me and scream, 'Batmama, Batmama!' so I thought, 'Wouldn't it be funny to have a pregnant superhero who saves children?'

"I try to match my pitch to the style of the script. For instance, for this one I usually do my opening spiel about the Batman glasses and then I announce in my best superhero voice: 'Devoted wife, mother of three, superhero! Finally a superhero that can change diapers!' Hopefully, I'll get a smile or a laugh. If I do, I continue. 'This is the story of Rhonda Brown, a mousy housewife who's cleaning her oven one day when she's hit by a bolt of lightning and transforms into...Batmommy! At exactly that moment, the diaper delivery man touches her hand and he's transformed into...Diaperman! Batmommy and Diaperman must save the little town of Shadyglade from the evil Dr. Rex A. Lynne, noted psychiatrist who is running for mayor and trying to take the *child* out of childhood.'

"I do the whole thing with as much enthusiasm and bravado as I can muster. This is where my years of acting school come in.

"I stop and wait. If the guy's not at least smiling, I'm dead. Not the right producer. I'll tell him so and try to see if there is something else I can get him interested in. But if I do get the smile or the laugh, I wait. I let the producer ask questions.

"I usually memorize my pitches, so I can take my attention off what I'm saying and watch the producer to see how it's going. I never continue when they've lost interest. If they're hooked, I shut up. If I see that I've lost them, I cop to it and ask them if they'd like to hear something else, or I leave gracefully. If they ask a few questions, I answer happily. If they ask too many questions, I figure I've lost them.

"Even if I don't think I have anything that would be good for a producer, I'll sit down and give them my resume and card anyway. I'll say that I don't think I have anything they want, but I like to write other people's projects, or work on rewrites or whatever — I sell the writer-for-hire angle. I try to get them to read a writing sample. I figure that maybe some day I'll write something that will be good for that producer, and they might remember me.

"Another important point: Never say anything nasty about anyone else in the business. I wrote a script with a partner that this actor/director made into a terrible movie, and then he said our script was bad on Howard Stern's radio show. He said he had to rewrite us. *Our* writing was bad! So this other producer looks at my resume and mentions this actor/director's name — notice how I've omitted it here, (see, I'm learning) — and I proceed to tell the producer what I thought of this guy. Well, it turns out the producer was working with him. So unless he shares my opinion, I look small and nasty.

"As an aside, I once asked a producer if he thought it was a disadvantage to be a female writer. He said he thought the best thing to be was a black, twenty-one-year-old lesbian. I said, 'That's amazing. I *am* black, twenty-one and a lesbian!' I've also heard more than a few times that producers want you to be young. So I wear sun block year round and

97

try and pass for mid-twenties even though I'm pushing mid-thirties — okay late-thirties. I don't think I've ever had a producer come right out and ask me my age, but I try to appear younger than *they* are. You can always *dress* the part even if you don't look it.

"Besides skirting the age issue, I don't let them know that I have another job besides writing. Even in the many, many years when I didn't make enough as a writer to pay for the paper I wrote on, I left the impression that it's the only job I do. Poverty-stricken is not some sort of bonus. I let them know that I'll write anything for anyone, as long as there's a paycheck involved. I don't write for free. On the other hand, I don't let them think I'm so well-off that I don't need them.

"Another thing: When Ken helped me write my resume, he had me write a line on the bottom of it that said, 'currently working on a spec script' — 'a' being the operative word. I don't let them know that in truth, I've got half a dozen scripts that have been lying around for years that I can't sell and haven't been optioned. I have one that I just finished — no one's seen it and it's the best one I've ever written. That's the one I'm pitching today. If I fall on my face but I get another chance, I can pitch one of my other half-dozen scripts, and say that it might be available or finished soon.

"My favorite part of the movie *The Player* is when the writers talk about their films in terms of other films. I, of course, do that. I tell the producer, tongue-in-cheek of course, that I've got *All That Jazz* meets *Friends* on *Fantasy Island*. Or I've got a John Hughes film from his *Say Anything* years. Or a *Free Willy*. In other words, a film that children will love and parents won't mind sitting through over and over. I try to look like I know something about the market, like I'm a well-established commercial writer. I wouldn't want anyone to think that they won't make money from one of my scripts.

"In terms of how all this pitching has worked out, I don't have the magic Hollywood story of the perfect pitch, instant option, million-dollar movie. I have a Rolodex of producers who like my style but what they've read so far 'isn't quite right.' They say they'll read my next script. Being the Pitch Queen doesn't mean I can't write. In fact, there are other writers in my writers' group who have had more scripts optioned and sold than I have, but they can't touch my numbers on getting reads. They are two separate skills, and you need both.

"One producer read one of my scripts, didn't like it, but didn't hate it enough not to read my superhero film. He took it all over town, and I got rejected by some of the biggest names in the business. I ended up writing the script with him for that loud-mouthed actor/director, and it ended up on the cable channel Showtime. I often tell producers that I wrote one of the worst movies ever shown on Showtime, just so they know that I've been produced. Even a bad movie credit means more than no credits at all!

"That same producer hired me to write another movie called *Land of the Free* with William Shatner and Jeff Speakman that was shown on HBO. He's now running around town with another script we wrote together. That doesn't stop my parents from wondering when I'm going to get a job. I think they'll wonder that even when I am nominated and get them tickets to the Academy Awards."

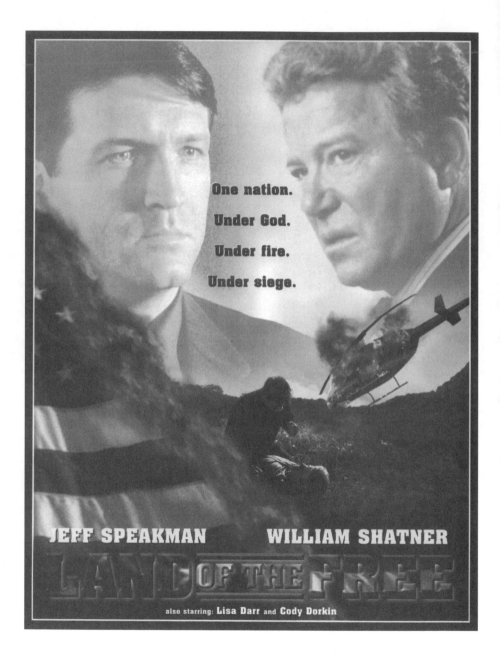

ATTACHMENTS
The Golden Key? Maybe.

Overheard at the Workshop:

"I had three scripts to pitch. One was a sci-fi, one was a western, one was a romantic comedy. Before I start, the executive says to me, 'No sci-fi, they're too expensive. No westerns, they're yesterday's news. And no romantic comedies, they're death in the foreign market. Okay, now, what have you got?' 'A headache,' I tell him."

Remember, the average executive hears hundreds of pitches each year. A very small percent are on ideas alone, with the script yet to be written. Most pitches are to get him to read existing scripts. They also might look at breakdowns (summaries) on five hundred to a thousand books in a year.

There are those in Hollywood who would have you believe that if you can attach an actor or a director of note to a project it will enhance the project. This works sometimes, but not all the time. Many producers have deals with actors and directors themselves, and are constantly looking for projects for them. If your project comes in attached, they may have to turn you down unless you can unravel your commitment with these people, so that the producer can bring his own people to the package.

There are very few actors or actresses who can "open" a picture, which means that based on their name alone, people will go see the film. No matter how good it is, how bad it is, how well it's been received, or how badly critics have panned it, there are enough fans of that actor to assure financial success.

A perfect example is Jim Carrey's *Me, Myself and Irene*, which got horrific reviews across the board and was even called a total embarrassment by some critics. Yet the picture was number one at the box office in the first week it came out, and eventually turned into a moneymaker. Jim Carrey can open a picture, any picture.

If you can get an actor who can open a picture, then you can use his name. And in most cases, you don't even have to go to a production company, you can go directly to a studio to get the financing to make the picture.

Everybody is looking for projects for the Harrison Fords, the Mel Gibsons, the Jim Carreys, the Tom Hankses or Tom Cruises of the world. If you can attract one of them to your script when you go in to pitch it, it almost doesn't matter what you say. They'll buy it based on the magnitude of the star.

Ironically, it does not work for actresses as much as it does for actors. Julia Roberts can open a picture. Goldie Hawn and Sandra Bullock would need a co-star with them. Even Meg Ryan and Michelle Pfeiffer, with their huge followings, would probably need a co-star. When you're talking feature films, it's really the actors who can open a film much more so than actresses. But all of this can change overnight. The industry and the public are so fickle.

Few directors are so well known that they can open a picture. With the exception of Steven Spielberg, you'd probably have to go back to Alfred Hitchcock to find a director the general audience knew and followed loyally. But within the industry, there are directors who have multi-deals with the studios, so having them attached to your project can guarantee you a deal.

Most producers think that ideas are cheap. They'd much rather have a script behind the pitch. For emerging writers, this is absolutely necessary. It's imperative that you have a script that your agent, manager or attorney can deliver if the producer likes your pitch.

When you become a writer of note, then you don't need a full script, and, in many cases, you don't even need to go in and take a meeting. You can simply pick up the phone and call your favorite producers or executives, and pitch the story over the phone and make a deal.

In the early days of television, a writer of note could also do that. He could call an executive for Movies of the Week at ABC, NBC or CBS, because of his reputation. The executive would say, "pitch it to me over the phone." The name writer would do so and then the executive would say, "That's great, let's make a deal. Do you have a production company tied into it?"

Of course, in most cases, they wouldn't. The executive would say, "Fine, we'll get you a production company for your project." That's how business was done. But, when the FCC found out that many of the executives were getting kickbacks from certain production companies for recommending them, the FCC put a halt to that system. Now writers must go to the production companies first. After they make a deal, the writer can go to one of the supervisors at one of the networks, or the cable companies, and pitch his movie. Now it is up to the writer to get a production company interested first, before the networks or cables will even meet with the writer.

Most spec scripts come from emerging writers trying to prove themselves, but now even a major writer will write something on spec, knowing they can get a lot more money on a spec script than they can if they develop it under the umbrella of a studio. A lot of well-known writers are turning more and more to the spec script.

In the old days, the studio would buy a lot of books, and then hand them out to writers to develop into screenplays. But the return proved to be unprofitable over the years, and cost the studios millions of dollars in books that simply could not be turned into screenplays. Finally, the studios said, "No more. We're better off buying spec scripts than we are books that have to be developed."

Today, studios buy very few books. Television does it more so now, because it's usually worth five points in the ratings to a network if they can have a Movie of the Week, either based on a real-life story or on a successful or popular book. A book written by a known writer, Danielle Steel for instance, guarantees success. It doesn't matter what she writes, the networks will buy it in a minute. They'll push Danielle Steel as their major selling point when they're promoting the movie.

In features, a spec script from an unknown writer can start as high as half a million dollars, and for a known writer three million dollars and up. You can see why more and more spec scripts are being written. The money is fantastic.

Try not to pitch something that's in vogue. In other words, if vampire movies are hot at the moment and you have a terrific vampire movie, the chances of it getting made are really very small, because by the time your story gets on film, the vampire craze is over.

But the film industry is very cyclical. What may be out of vogue today may be back in vogue in five or six years. Keep your story handy, wait until that particular subject is out of fashion and that's the time to pitch it. Samuel Goldwyn, the studio mogul, used to say, "When they're not making Westerns, that's when I want to make a Western."

Today the buzz is romantic comedy. For one thing, you don't have to get great reviews to draw an audience. Moreover, shooting a romantic comedy is not expensive. Of course, this too will be cyclical. World War II stories that were verboten for so many years have come back and are now in vogue.

At the moment, nostalgia is out, but by the time this book comes out, nostalgia may be back in. With the high cost of making films, it's easier to make a present-day story than one that requires period costumes, tracking down vintage cars, and finding cities that do not have modern buildings to clutter up the screen.

There is another theory which states that, by and large, the audience for motion pictures is the teen-youth market. The theory goes that the American teen-youth market of today has no understanding of, nor respect for, history. And doesn't want to learn it. They want escapist fare; they don't want to think or feel they're being lectured to. It reminds them of going to school.

There is also something that writers call the script detective. The script detective is the underpaid assistant to the executive who gets to sit in on these meetings, and is looking for loopholes in your story so he can jump in and show everyone how bright and clever he is. He is merely demonstrating to his boss that he's worth the underpayment he is receiving. These people are a pain in the neck. They're overly aggressive and trying desperately to score points at your expense. Be prepared to have answers for the holes that these script detectives find. However, don't blow it by coming up with something on the spur of the moment which may not work. If you don't know the answer, say to the executive, "Gee, that's a good point. I hadn't thought about it. I don't have an answer, but if I may, I'll call you tomorrow and tell you how I would respond to that."

When Pitching Gets Scary

You can pitch the heck out of your story and get an executive very, very excited. He now must either go to the head of his company or directly to the studio or network to pitch that story for you. Many times executives don't invite the writer to come along. They want to do it on their own.

There are a few reasons why they do this. First it's because they may have more than one project to pitch and they don't want to bring in a room full of writers all sitting around waiting their turn. The producer will do the pitching for all the projects.

Second, he may have a personal relationship with the producer that he's not interested in exposing to you at this time.

And third, the producer may be on an ego trip, and he wants the spotlight solely on himself, not on the writer he brings along.

You're now at the mercy of the producer taking your story and pitching it to somebody else. That person will in turn probably have to go and pitch it to his boss, and up the ladder it goes. Therefore, it may be to your advantage to write that synopsis, and God knows I hate synopses, but sometimes they give the executive the ammunition he needs to properly pitch your material. He has something to refer to when you're not there.

A lot of writers will break the synopsis down to three acts, just as you would a screenplay. It makes it easier to follow, and it shows the executive, in fact, that you understand the formula of writing. The synopsis should be one page long, and not any longer, because inevitably if it's two pages, I can guarantee you the executive will lose the second page.

Secondly, the synopsis should be written in the same style as the screenplay. (A comedy must be funny, etc.) This is very tough. Instead of giving a synopsis, I'd rather give them the first ten pages of my script. I bind it, just the way I would a full screenplay and give it to the executive to pass up the line. The hope is that the people who read those ten pages will:

  a) get a feeling for my material, and
  b) get a feeling that I can write, and
  c) get to understand and meet my protagonist,
      my antagonist, and see what the conflict is
      between the two of them.

A good screenplay should have all of that in the first ten pages. If I can get an executive to read those first ten pages, I'm convinced I can hook them enough to read the rest of my script.

CONTESTS
The Big Four, Plus Two, Plus One, and a New One.

Overheard at the Workshop:

"I joined Ken's Workshop because I was told if you want to learn how to pitch, he's the guy to see. A few weeks later, I met the girl of my dreams. After we dated a while, I proposed. Well, not exactly proposed, rather I pitched her on why she should marry me. She said yes! Damn, that Rotcop's good!"

There really is a terrific way to get your screenplay into the right hands. Enter it in a contest. The judges are made up of executives in the industry, some representing studios, some representing literary agencies, others production companies. All these companies are open to scripts that have placed well in a contest.

There are six major screenwriting contests that I recommend highly. You can consider sending your screenplays to them. They do not require pitching. They do not require a query letter. They simply ask you to fill out an application, submit your script, and a check for a readers' fee, which runs from thirty to forty-five dollars.

There is always the chance that you might be a winner. In many cases, they give money to the winner as well as to the second and third runner-up. Or, you may be given a year at a studio to further develop that script. Another prize might be an opportunity to write your next script while on salary.

There are dozens of lesser screenplay contests. Most of them are held away from the spotlight of Hollywood, and are really of little benefit to the winner except that you might get a check, in many cases for five hundred to one thousand dollars. Although you certainly can list on your resume having won or been runner-up in some of these contests.

The six big contests pay up to $33,000 for first prize.

The interesting thing we've discovered about these contests is the fact that the best scripts don't always win, but the winning scripts are always quite good. Because industry executives sit on the panels, they very often read a script and fall in love with it. If this is the case, they'll find out the name of the writer and try to take the script out of competition and option it.

In fact, three Workshop members have been contacted by jurists, who wanted to take the script out of the competition because they wanted to option it.

In all these situations, the writers came to me and asked what they should do. Should they stay in the competition where they might win first prize of $30,000, or should they option it?

I must say that each case was individual. In two of the three cases, the executives that wanted to option the scripts were very reputable and had done some good work. In those situations, it was thought best to have them optioned, even though the option money was less than the first-prize money.

Why not wait until the winner was announced? Because it's months and months from the time of the deadline until the winners are announced. Our two writers were anxious to get going.

In the third case, we checked on the credentials of the producer. I did not personally know him. His credentials were minimal at best and it was decided to leave the script in competition, where it did reach the semi-finals.

Generally, for an unknown or wannabe producer, let him wait until the contest is over.

Many contests now require that your name not appear on the script. (It appears only on the application form.) Each script is coded with a number. This supposedly eliminates favoritism and keeps executives from taking scripts out of the competition.

But entering contests is a great way to have your screenplay get exposure. It *will* open doors for you. Many of these contests will contact you to tell you whether your script is still in the running after the quarter-finals, semi-finals, or finals, and of course, when you're an award-winner.

If you reach at least the semi-finals of a major contest, put it on your resume. It is a strong indication as to the quality of your work.

Should you move up the ladder of a major contest, there is a good chance that an agency that is represented on the panel will ask you to become a client. Or, some producer or executive may option your material, if not during the contest, then when the contest is over and all the names are revealed.

I've included this chapter in a book on pitching screenplays because it's one of the best shortcuts I know of for getting exposure for your material. It's the only time a pitch is *not* required.

I will tell you a secret. The jurists who take home piles of scripts to read are *human*, so it better be exciting. Again, quickly establish the premise of your story, who your protagonist is, what it is that he wants and who's stopping him from getting it. And remember, do this all within the first ten pages. They've got a lot to read in a short time so if you don't grab them in the first ten pages, your chance of winning them over is almost nonexistent.

There is one exception, where you'll want to have your pitch down pat. That's if you apply for one of the Disney/ABC Studio Fellowships. (The ABC Studio half is for TV writers). When Disney goes through some 4,000 scripts and it gets down to the finalists, they are so concerned with the character of the individual writers, they will interview each of the finalists. That means you need the ability to pitch.

This fellowship is one year of salaried employment (currently $33,000). So again, it's a question of "Is this someone we want to work with?"

The interview is also to determine if you are a worthy individual to represent Disney outside of the studio. If you win, you might be asked to do interviews, for instance, or make personal appearances on Disney's behalf.

Yes, Disney will ask you to pitch your material. They will ask you a lot of questions about how you came up with the concept and the story. They may also want to know what your next projects might be.

They are one of the few studios that will give you office space, assign a producer to you and give you a salary. They will give you one year to work on your next project, under the auspices of a Disney producer, with the thought that Disney will produce your next screenplay if they don't buy the one that you've entered in the competition.

Here are the names of the six major competitions:
These four are located in the greater Hollywood area.

1.   The Nicholl Fellowships (Academy of Motion Picture Arts and Sciences). Up to five writers will receive a one-year fellowship of $25,000. Deadline: Early May.
        Contact: *nicholl@oscars.org*

2.   The Disney Studio/ABC TV Fellowships: Eight writers in features and TV shall be employed for one year with a $33,000 salary. Deadline: Mid-May.
        Contact: (818) 560-6894

3.   The Chesterfield Film Company's Film Project, up to five writers receive a stipend of $20,000. Deadline: October. Contact: *www.chesterfield-co.com*

4.   The Diane Thomas Award (Open only to students of UCLA's undergraduate, graduate school, or Extension Division writing programs).
Contact: (310) 206-1145

The two most respected contests outside of the area are:

5.   Sundance Feature Film Project. Deadline: Early May. Contact: *www.sundanceresort.com*

6.   Austin "Heart of Film" Screenplay Competition (Part of the Austin Film Festival). Deadline: Mid-May. Contact: *www.austinfilmfestival.com*

One other contest worth mentioning is the Final Draft "Big Break" Competition. It's new in this form, as of the year 2000, and offers cash prizes to the top five winners. $10,000 to First, $6,000 to Second, $3,000 to Third, $2,000 to Fourth and $1,000 to Fifth. Because it is new, I can't endorse it. Enter at your own risk. Early Deadline: May 20. Late Deadline: Sept. 20. Contact: *www.finaldraft.com*

Just as we were finishing this book, a new and very exciting contest was announced. Project Greenlight was launched in the fall of 2000 by Miramax, HBO, Matt Damon, Ben Affleck, and Chris Moore.

Any U.S. resident over 18 can submit a screenplay online to *www. projectgreenlight.com*. There is NO ENTRY FEE! While there isn't a charge for entering the contest, each submitting writer must agree to critique three scripts.

The winner gets to direct his or her film, which is financed by Miramax with a $1 million budget. Executive producers are Damon, Affleck, and

111

Moore. HBO plans a 13-episode documentary-style TV series on the making of the movie, which will begin airing in January 2002.

For current information on all contests go to *www.moviebytes.com*.

PITCHING EXPERIENCES
OF WORKSHOP MEMBERS
One-on-one with Producers and Executives.

Overheard at the Workshop:

"I'm sitting across from this very attractive producer, and as I start my pitch, I can see he's checking me out. Just as I'm getting to the first act turning point, he interrupts me. 'How would you like to have dinner with me next week?' Flattered, I say 'yes,' and continue my story.

"When I'm finished, he says, 'Better yet, I have a condo in Telluride. Do you ski?' Now, I'm thinking, he must really like my pitch if he's asking me go out of town with him. As I get up to leave, I ask, 'So what did you think of my story?' And with a lecherous wink he answers, 'What story? I'll call you tomorrow about this weekend.' I can't wait for his call, so I can say, 'What producer?'"

In the lead-in to the song, "Getting to Know You," from *The King and I*, is the line: "If you become a teacher, by your pupils you'll be taught." Here are some of the experiences from members of my Professional Writers Workshop. Remember, their experiences are based on Pitchmarts, where we bring twenty-five executives from studios, networks, and production companies together to meet exclusively, one-on-one, with the writers from my Workshop.

"The funniest pitch that I had, was this production company that wanted a reality-based comedy. Their table was empty, so I walked over and said, 'I've got a comedy, but it's not reality-based.' They said, 'Well, go ahead and pitch it.' I sat down and I pitched it. They weren't interested. Not for them at all. 'What else have you got?'

"I started pitching a serious piece, but I forgot to tell them it was serious. I'm pitching this serious thing, and they think it's a comedy, and they're

113

rolling on the floor...'and the creatures come back to life' (laugh), 'and the monster comes at them,' (laugh). When they finally realized it was a serious piece, they were terribly embarrassed. But I found the whole thing uproarious. And no, I cannot rewrite it as a comedy, it simply wouldn't work."

Lesson: Always tell them the genre first.

■ ■ ■

"The most frustrating one I had, I started this pitch, I just got to the premise and the guy says, 'Stop! I want to read the script, and I want it right away!' Wonderful! And then he didn't return my calls for six months. I finally got the script back in the mail, unopened!"

Lesson: Beware of executives who don't return your phone calls for six months. If they haven't been fired, they should be.

■ ■ ■

"When you go to one of Ken's Pitchmarts, you receive a list of the participants. The printed material says they're looking for a murder mystery, and I've got the perfect thing. I come in all charged up, and then they said, 'No that's not what we're looking for.' I said, 'Aren't you looking for a murder mystery?' 'No.' It just sort of throws you and you just go blank.

"So now, I ask first, 'What are you really looking for?' If they're not specific, I'll ask, 'Are you looking for a murder mystery, a supernatural thriller, are you looking for this, or for that?' Then they'll say, 'Tell me about your supernatural thriller.' That's what I found works the best."

Lesson: Always find out what they're interested in or what they're looking for, before you pitch.

■ ■ ■

"One of the executives mentioned the word, 'expansive.' 'We are looking for an expansive story.' So, I sat down and I said, 'Here's a thing that I have, it's really expansive. That's the one he wanted to see. I even pitched it badly. I know it was a bad pitch. But, because I clued in on his words, he said. 'Yeah, I'd like to see that one.'"

Lesson: Listen to what they say, then paraphrase them to catch their interest.

■ ■ ■

"I did a pitch to an executive from United Paramount Network (UPN) and I got this guy's energy level, I know what he's like. I feel I've got him! Also, I worked for Paramount Pictures, so I got to see a couple of their movies.

"I sit down and I say, 'Hey, I've worked for Paramount and I've seen a couple of your movies.' The guy goes, 'Wow, that's great. How did you like [xxx]?' I say, 'What?' I had no idea what he was talking about. I leaped in with the right energy, but then immediately thought, 'Oh, no, I screwed up.' I completely shut down. And, of course, the pitch was doomed."

Lesson: Don't try to con a professional by saying you've seen something you haven't. It's certain to backfire.

■ ■ ■

"Several producers will come up to you in the middle of a pitch and say 'Well, this sounds like such and such a movie. Have you seen that movie?' If you say, 'No, I haven't seen such and such a movie.' They'll say, 'Wait a minute, you haven't seen this movie?! But you're writing something like it. Why haven't you seen this movie?' Then you have to come up with a quick response.

"That's exactly what happened to me. I started to pitch this idea and he said, 'Did you see such and such movie?' And I say, 'No, I didn't.' He got very mad. He said you should see movies. I said, 'I see movies, I just didn't see that one.' 'Well, you should, it's your story.' I felt devastated.

I thought, 'Oh my God, my story has already been done.' So the next day I went out and I looked at the movie, and it was nothing at all like the story that I'm writing."

Lesson: A lot of uncreative producers need to immediately find a niche for your story. Remember, they're thinking grosses so if they can compare your story to a big moneymaker, they'll be more interested.

▬ ▬ ▬

"A major production company I knew wouldn't buy this particular screenplay, but I wanted to pitch it to her anyway. She agreed to listen and says, 'You know, I wish we could do something with that, it sounds like a great story. I know we can't make it, but I'd like to read it.' That told me I had a great pitch.

"I brought enthusiasm to it, and when she leaves that company, she may take it with her. That's the other reason why you want to pitch to everybody. Give them everything, whether they're ready to buy it or not. Just get it out there, because you never know, they may just say 'yes' somewhere down the road — and it might very well be at a different production company."

Lesson: Remember, in any form of sales, it's a numbers game. Don't get discouraged. Every "no" brings you closer to the final "yes."

▬ ▬ ▬

"One of the first times I did a pitch, it was a script with a sports background, although it's not actually about sports. As I was pitching, I noticed that the guys were into it and the women's eyes were glazing over. Yet, it was a movie that could appeal to women as well.

"I began to realize that the way I was pitching it was more geared towards sports because I figured that would be more well received. My advice to anyone who is planning to pitch a sports-related movie: first find out the sex of the person who will be making the final decision. I did encounter some women who, even though they weren't interested in it themselves said, 'Yeah, our boss loves sports.' So in that regard it worked out."

Lesson: Pitch chick flicks to women, jock flicks to men.

■ ■ ■

"It's odd how mercurial producers are. From one extreme to the other. In one pitch for a supernatural sci-fi story, I was actually taking on the role of the villain.

"I did the final line in the voice of this monster. Then, in a normal voice, I asked if they were interested or had any questions. Every time I pitched it, I was told it was a great pitch. They may not necessarily want the story, but they loved that pitch.

"One producer, who teaches a seminar on pitching, gave me her card and wanted me to come in and demonstrate the pitch to her class.

"In another instance, I did the pitch and ended by asking the producer if he had any questions. The guy just chuckled and said, 'Are you a wannabe actor?'

"After an entire day of successes, I was thrown by his reaction. I was thinking, 'Whoa, I wasn't expecting that.' He was completely turned off by the way I delivered my pitch.

"But don't let one person discourage you. There's nothing you can do about it. Just accept it and go on. You really have to be thick-skinned in this business, if you want to be successful. You will get advice from producers on what to pitch or how to pitch. Be gracious, because it may be good advice from people who hear pitches all the time.

"On the other hand, it's not the be all and end all. It's not gospel. It is not, 'You absolutely must change this.' But listen to what they have to say, you might learn something."

Lesson: No matter what you do, some people aren't going to get it. Just thank them and press on to the next opportunity.

■ ■ ■

"The very first Pitchmart I went to, I didn't have anything to pitch, but I wanted to learn how. I went to the Workshop for maybe two weeks before the Pitchmart. I told Ken I was just going to go and listen to everybody else pitch, so that I could learn how to do it.

"But I lucked out, because another writer came and she said, 'Listen, I have to be out of town that day. I was wondering if there was anybody here who could read my scripts and pitch them for me?' I said, 'Sure, no problem.' Then if it was a disaster, I'm not losing anything. If I'm good, I'm helping her out, so we both win.

"I read both her scripts and pitched both of them. What a great way to learn how to pitch, if you can possibly do it. You read somebody else's work and pitch it, but you're also getting the hang of it without that personal emotional stake in it the first time. So, I highly recommend that."

Lesson: Pitching for someone else can reduce the anxiety, and aid in overcoming any fear of pitching.

■ ■ ■

"At my first Pitchmart, I was a disaster. But one of the key things I learned that day was you have to sit through a few before you get the hang of it. No matter how much you prepare for it. I felt kind of bad about it, but then, later that day I was getting good reception, so I knew that I was on the mark."

Lesson: If you attend a pitch session, don't start with the executive you want most to hear your pitch. Choose a few that you don't give a damn about and practice with them to get warmed up.

■ ■ ■

"I have to tell you my experience of pitching over a phone. I had a contact who put me on the line to Canada with the production company who did the CBS Joan of Arc. I got her on the phone and said I wanted to send her my script. She was in development, and told me, 'If you want us to take the script, you've got to get an agent.' I said, 'By the time I get an agent, it just won't be fresh.' She said, 'Tell me what it is.' So I bumbled my way into it. Then finally she said, 'Just send me a synopsis.'

"I sent her a synopsis and then she calls me back and said, 'I wanted to tell you, I took your synopsis and I discussed it at a board meeting. They said it's just not the type of story that we're interested in doing at this time. But I think it was very good and I'm sorry that we had to pass on it.' This is the big lesson, within a year another producer fell madly in love with my story. Then he went to work for that company who had passed on my story. Within the same year, that producer went to the same board meeting, pitched the same story, same characters, they loved it and they optioned it.

"What I get now is, it's not always the message, but it's the messenger."

Lesson: If you can find someone with enough clout in the industry to champion your work, that can be the golden key.

■ ■ ■

"I wrote a script about the meeting at Yalta with Roosevelt, Churchill, and Stalin. I went with a production company. They pitched it to CBS and they turned it down. The production company said, 'No use taking it to ABC or NBC because this isn't the kind of thing they do. It's a CBS-type project and if they turned it down, you're dead in the water.'

"So I took it away from them and went to another production company. This company said. 'Why don't you take it to CBS? I didn't say anything. So they took it to CBS and had the same results.

"Now a few weeks go by, and I'm at a party and I meet a man from another production company who asks, 'What are you working on?' I tell him my story about the Nazis trying to assassinate the men at Yalta. He said, 'Boy, that's a CBS movie. Why don't you take it over to CBS?' I said, 'Yeah, I'd love to but...' The guy says, 'No, no, no!' and he takes it through his company, and CBS buys it.

"All that happened in a matter of six weeks. Now, what happened in that time? I can only guess. CBS has five different executives who are supervisors. I learned that each production company, and there are dozens, reports to one of the five. What two supervisors couldn't get through, the third one did.

"So it got turned down twice by CBS, and bought by CBS, and yet the boss had never seen it until the third supervisor said, 'Yeah, I want to do this project.' When you get turned down by a company, what I've learned is go to another company. If they report to a different supervisor from the first, it's a whole new game!"

Lesson: In the words of *Galaxy Quest*, "Never give up! Never surrender!"

■ ■ ■

"I have an embarrassing situation. The first time I gave a pitch, an executive said, 'Okay, send me the script.' He also said, 'But I'm very heavily involved with post production on... [a major feature], so it will be a while before I can get to this.' Thrilled at the opportunity of having an executive read my material, I, of course, said, 'That's fine.'

"A couple of months passed, but I knew they were still in post, so I didn't want to be a bother. Then six months had gone by, and I didn't feel comfortable asking, 'Did you read it, did you read it?' So I let it slip. Now three years have gone by, and I'm way too embarrassed to bring the subject up."

Lesson: Once you have sent your script to an executive, it's part of your job to stay on top of your project. Give them three weeks, then, at the very least, confirm that they have received it. If they haven't read it yet, ask when it would be an appropriate time for you to follow up. Whenever possible, don't leave it for them to call you. You call them!

PITCHES THAT HAVE SOLD
Success Stories from Workshop Members.

Overheard at the Workshop:

"This producer takes me to lunch and says, 'I wanted to meet you to tell you how much we all loved your screenplay.' I manage to grunt a thank you because my mouth is filled with Mahi-Mahi.

"'Unfortunately,' he continues, 'your story isn't quite right for my company, but because the writing is so strong, I'd like to pitch you three ideas to see if you'd like to write a script for one of our stories.'

"While I'm disappointed they're not going to buy mine, I'm elated that they want to hire me to do one of theirs.

"Between bites of his lobster salad, he pitches three stories to me. They're awful, each one worse than the next. I shake my head no to the first, the second and the third story. I hated them all.

"I can see he's hurt and disappointed. I feel bad until I'm in my car and review the lunch meeting.

"I had just knocked myself out of a writing assignment, but...I had turned him down! I had made him feel bad! I had ruined his lunch. I had made him feel unworthy, uncreative, destroyed his confidence and tore great holes in his stories, ruining them forever. For the coup de grace, I told him his pitching sucked! God, what a great lunch!"

In recent years a staggering *fifteen* projects, including screenplays and plays for the theatre, have actually been produced out of my Workshop and Pitchmart. At one point, each of these had to be pitched. What did these winning pitches actually sound like? Were they magical?

123

Follow along as I take you on a few successful odysseys, starting with a pitch and ending with either a movie made or a play produced.

JIM FRAZIER

Jim Frazier is the only person to win the prestigious Carl Sautter Memorial Screenwriting Award two years in a row. In 1999, he won best screenplay for *Mr. Madden* (with co-writer Julian McGrath) and in 2000 he won for *Last Buffalo Hunter*.

He also was selected as a semi-finalist for the 2000 Nicholl Fellowship, sponsored by the Academy of Motion Picture Arts and Sciences, for *Last Buffalo Hunter*.

His latest science fiction blockbuster, *The God Cell*, which he co-authored with his wife, Laura, was selected winner of the 2000 New Century Writer Award.

"I recently negotiated a seven-figure deal, based on just a pitch. But even if you have a great pitch, and have won a number of awards, producers still want to see a writing sample that will blow them away, especially if you're not an established writer. When I pitched *Legion*, I already had forty-seven pages of the screenplay written, plus nine pages of the treatment. I also had a good writing sample. It was a script for a movie bigger than the one I pitched, and it was 130 pages long. That's how hard it is to convince them you're real.

"When you're talking about a large, one-hundred-million-dollar studio picture, they need to see that it's a lot more than just a sexy idea. With the proliferation of screenwriting software, anybody can come to the studio with a great concept. It's the delivery, the execution of that idea, that they're concerned about.

"Pitching a concept today is different than it was ten years ago when there weren't as many writers hawking their stories. Back then, if somebody pitched something and a studio liked it, they would develop it. Now, producers have become much more cautious, especially if someone is an unknown quantity, because the screenplay doesn't always live up to the pitch. Your script must be killer. You must prove you can write.

"If you're going to pitch an over-the-top science fiction story, don't give them a writing sample of something charming, personal and intimate. They'll wonder what the hell you're doing. They might even like it. Most likely, they'll tell you to go home and write the screenplay they were expecting, then come back and talk.

"I could never have sold the pitch if I didn't have a similar story of the same magnitude and style to show that I understood what they were looking for.

"Major players at the studios are different than independent producers. They're looking for a poster. They're looking for high-concept that will captivate them just by the log line. They want big, visual, instantly commercial projects. If you're not writing that kind of script, chances are you're wasting their time.

"My film *Legion* is a good example. Imagine during annual war games, 1,000 miles off the coast of Hawaii. The leader of the Navy Seals is Sylvester Stallone. The leader of the Army Rangers is Arnold Schwarzenegger. During the exercise, a massive earthquake sheers the crust of the earth and a demon army from hell escapes prematurely and lands on this island. The army has been assigned to go forth and destroy the world at the end of the age. Our heroes must conquer them, becoming, the first, last, and only hope for mankind's survival.

"That's the poster. That's my million-dollar pitch. The movie's huge, you can instantly see the trailer, the poster, the one-sheet.

"Another high-concept movie I found easy to pitch was *Hell's Fire*. Spontaneous human combustion was such a novel idea, the minute I told the producers what it was about, they said they'd read it.

"I purposely set out to write a script that could become a franchise picture, a concept that would generate a series of sequels. I also picked a subject that had never been done on the big screen. Similar things had been done on videos, but not as a big-budget feature film.

"Too often, novice writers do stories that are too esoteric, like growing up in Fresno. Those ideas are not going to appeal to a major studio. Who wants to spend as much as eleven dollars, plus the cost of a baby-sitter, to see people running through orchards? The general public doesn't care about your upbringing in Fresno. They want to see Arnold Schwarzenegger and Sylvester Stallone beat each other. If they're going to spend money, they want to be thrown into a world within an inch of death. Unlike theirs, a world where they can fantasize, projecting themselves into something grand.

"Writing 'small' limits you to the financially strapped independent market. However, if you want to write for the studio market and be successful, you've got to write *BIG*, high-concept stories. Once you're established, they'll want to see your smaller pictures. This is happening to me. I have three scripts that can be made for less than five million dollars each and I'm getting tremendous interest in them because of my big studio deal. It's sad, because those scripts were good before, but the perception of them has now changed.

"You've got to know the audience you're pitching to. Early on, I remember pitching a 60-million-dollar movie to companies that made two-million-dollar movies and had no previous screen credits. At the time, I innocently thought, 'What am I doing wrong?' In hindsight, it was great practice, but I was very naive, talking to people who had difficulty paying their phone bills.

"You've got to hone your craft. Ken taught me just how important editing is in the writing process. A story really blossoms when it's being rewritten. I spent the entire summer of 1999 rewriting six of my eight scripts. I was sowing seeds for when the big day comes. I knew I was up for the Carl Sautter Screenwriting Award. I didn't know if I was going to win, but if I did, I thought I'd better be ready.

"The first script I brought to Ken was a screenplay based on the classic Eagles song, 'Hotel California,' which has a lot of sex appeal. Ken, Julian, and I worked on it for a good six months. We cut out ten or twelve pages, all the stuff that beginners write like, 'we see..., we hear...,' all the junk that would embarrass me today. The revised script won the 1997 Roosevelt Screenwriting Competition and subsequently sold in 1998 in the mid to low six figures.

"Another important aspect of my writing career has been writing competitions. I don't go after every award, only those like the Nicholl or the Sautter, that mean something to studio people. These can really help your career because they give you an air of legitimacy. They also keep you going, because they give you inspiration. You may never sell anything directly as a result, but they reaffirm you and get you to stay in the game a little longer.

"Ken was heavily involved in three films that went on to do great things for my career and I attribute that to Ken's editing. As I've said before, even with a good pitch, you have to hand them material that is solid and professional.

"Your script has got to shout from that pile on the executive's desk! To make it shout, it's got to be different in such a way that it's going to get you talked about. Find that difference! I knew that it was just a matter of time if I worked hard enough. You've got to have a commitment from yourself and your family. I work part-time, I have investments which bring in some money, and my wife works part-time. This is a collective family vision and enterprise. It requires all pulling together in order to be successful."

MEG THAYER

Meg Thayer wrote and directed *True Rights*, which has won five awards:

Audience Award — Dances With Films — June 2000
Best Feature/New Vision — Brooklyn Film Festival — August 2000
Best Director — Brooklyn Film Festival — August 2000
Best Actor (Jack Betts) — Brooklyn Film Festival — August 2000
Best Feature/Narrative Category — Cinewomen Awards — September 2000

"Incredibly, the difference between a script and a 'go project,' may merely be someone declaring, 'Let's do it.' My great uncle Hez Namminga was this cool, congenial Dutch farmer who was never interested in spending money. In an effort to distribute his assets before he died, he gave me $7,000. That got the ball rolling. I dedicated the movie to him.

"I decided I was going to shoot *True Rights* on video. I wrote what I felt was a strong script, working for a year and a half on it, between other writing assignments. Then I basically told everyone 'I'm making a movie,' and the project became like a moving train. The momentum just kept building.

"Suddenly, a friend who worked for a commercial company said, 'Bring it over. We'll give you some more money and let's do it on film.' Then my husband (entertainment lawyer Leon Gladstone) contacted his childhood friend David Darby, who is a big commercial director of photography, and David came on board, bringing with him all sorts of crew, equipment and favors.

"Then Jeff Zacha of Disney came on board as Executive Producer and brought Soundelux in as a partner and suddenly everything about post-production became very easy. He was a true Godfather on the project.

"I must be honest, I didn't have to pitch my story. What I would pitch was who was attached, who was committed, and who was working with us. Then I would just hand out the script.

"When I was pitching to money people, they just wanted to know how I could do this project for a reasonable budget. I'd say, 'It's an easy script to shoot. It's all single camera, handheld. It's got David Darby; you can't go wrong. It's going to look good. I've got Claudia Christian, who is a very well-known sci-fi actress. She's going to work for a SAG limited exhibition rate, which is very little money. And the Jackson brothers (Richard Lee Jackson and Jonathan Jackson) were a big score. These actors turn in fearless, brilliant performances in *True Rights* that are completely 'against type.' I think I can speak for them when I say that part of their motivation was to stretch their legs as actors; to flex their muscles. Also, all of the main actors were very script-motivated.

"But when you're trying to raise money, it's irrelevant what the script or the story is. Probably more often than not. When you're actually getting to the point where someone is going to have to plunk down money, it becomes a question of who's involved. Who else is coming to the party?

"It's a good lesson to writers who think all they have to do is write a really beautiful, good story that speaks from the heart. Not true! I know a guy who got a writing job recently with a company that specializes in film sales in foreign markets. They said, 'We need a lesbian sex scene, x number of battles, and x amount of chases and explosions.' How weird is that?! It could be set in medieval England or apocalyptic Los Angeles. They didn't care. So, what's your pitch then?

"When I was in Ken's workshop, my writing partner Yves Martin and I sold a script called *Hidden Assassin*, which was released by Miramax. We had written it as a political thriller.

"They cast Dolph Lundgren and they brought in another writer and changed it completely. Now it's an action video you can rent at

Blockbuster. We made money and it's had good foreign sales, but it wasn't what we wrote at all.

"As for *True Rights*, it's really edgy. It's very hard-hitting and the characters are as vulgar as they can possibly be. There were people telling me not to make the movie myself but to sell it to a studio. I thought, 'Not on your life,' because what I wrote won't exist anymore.

"I'm not financially motivated. I can get by on a subsistence level. I didn't let go of it, because I didn't want it to be softened. I had a point that I wanted to make about true-story acquisitions and the sale of graphic video to news programs and video producers. We've all seen those 'real footage' exploitation videos at our local store.

"*True Rights* focuses on the middle men — the guys who bring this video footage onto our television sets as news clips or TV dramatizations or rentable exploitation videos. It's a subject I feel very strongly about and I didn't want it to be soft-pedaled.

"It all started when I read a column by Howard Rosenberg in *The Los Angeles Times*. It was about a couple that got a call in the middle of the night from an L.A. Sheriff's deputy. The deputy told them their son had been found dead of a drug overdose. They cried and carried on the way you would if you'd lost a child, not knowing that their call was being recorded or that the discovery of the dead son had been videotaped.

"One day the mother was doing housework and had the TV on in the background. On the cop show that was playing, she saw her son's dead body and cops milling around. Then she heard her and her husband's crying and hysteria when they received the news of their son's death. She was devastated. Someone was making money from having filmed her grief and her sorrow.

"Of course, the show was repeated despite the family's pleas and efforts to stop it.

"It energized me to write the script that exposes the type of people who would exploit human tragedy this way. And there was no other way to write it but as a comedy/satire, otherwise it would be just too distasteful — too brutal. The characters were too vulgar. Laughter was the spoonful of sugar that helped the medicine go down.

"I attended several of the Pitchmarts, and Ken will tell you, I'm not great at pitching. I've worked on it and I've gotten a little bit better, but the fact of the matter is, I really struggle with pitching. I'm not a sales-person, I'm a worker like my Dutch uncle Hez.

"So pitching is something Ken worked a lot on with me. There are some people who are naturally good at it; I'm not one of those people. I don't love to pitch.

"If I was going to pitch my story, it would go something like this."

TRUE RIGHTS

True Rights is a black comedy satire about Real TV and an eccentric crew of video vultures who sweep through Los Angeles trying to get the rights to the next great shock TV story. While they're out chasing ambulances and crashing crime scenes, they run into an old Hollywood silent-era actor who jokingly claims that he's going to commit suicide. If they want an exclusive story they can follow him. Then it becomes sort of a team moral crisis. They start turning against each other. At the end, it packs a punch that I can't give away.

"That's it. Man, I hate pitching."

JOHN McGOWAN

"I wrote an original script in Ken's workshop called *Paper Dog*, the true story of a German Shepherd War Dog in Vietnam. I went all over town with it and it never really got anywhere because a lot of studios felt it wasn't big enough for the screen, so I rewrote it with a new story and renamed it *Rain*, then shelved it for about eight years.

"Then in March of 1999, I saw a documentary on the Discovery Channel about the War Dogs in Vietnam. I called Ken to ask if he could help me pitch *Rain*. He suggested I attend the Pitchmart in two months. When I arrived at the Pitchmart, Ken said he picked up a cassette that was a promotional gimmick at a pet store, and it was a documentary about war dogs. And one of the stories was about 'Paper,' the subject of my original script. Clearly, the timing was right to make a story about a war dog.

"Just before the Pitchmart began, Ken and I were reminiscing, and as we were talking, one of the executives came by and Ken told her the story. She said, 'Stop by and see me and we'll talk more about it.'

"Also, Ken told me to use the cassette as a gimmick in telling my story, so he gave me the tape and I used it in my pitch. Ken is really good with suggestions like that. I also remember him saying, 'John, if we don't get this made, I'm leaving the entertainment business. I cannot believe this hasn't been made yet.'

"The Pitchmart started and over twenty executives and producers were there. I pitched to about sixteen of them. Twelve wanted to see the script, but I knew a few of those wouldn't be a good fit when it came to a working relationship.

"Then I went back to the first woman Ken and I talked to, and she said, 'Of course, I want to read it.' A week later she called, 'It's fantastic. I love the script and I have a friend at the Animal Planet Channel who's looking for these kinds of projects.'

"The Animal Planet, under the Discovery Channel umbrella, was doing feature films on animals, so it was the right time, the right place. That executive read my script and moved it right up the ladder at Discovery. Everybody loved it and they wanted to use it as their showcase movie to launch their programs about animals.

"Here's the pitch that had those twelve executives asking for the screenplay."

RAIN
(THE STORY OF A WAR DOG)

This is the story of a German Shepherd named Rain, owned by a little girl, who gave up her precious animal to the army, so it could be trained to become one of the most elite fighting dogs in the history of dog training. The heart of the story is about this dog and its handler as they lead a recon platoon through the jungles of Vietnam. Rain helped save hundreds of U.S. soldiers. These dogs are the true unsung heroes of Vietnam.

"That's pretty much how it went down. That short, that quick. Then the executives would asked questions.

"The war dogs' story has never really been told. Very few people know that war dogs existed. That's why it's such a good hook.

"It took me a while to find something to write about in Ken's class. It had to be high-concept, something with a real good hook and angle to it. It was a pretty difficult story to write because the dog is the main character. It was difficult to make it realistic and not dopey. I didn't want to write another *Lassie*.

"It has elements that are edgy, but just enough, so it's not *Platoon*. It's not *Lassie* but it's in between the two.

"The Pitchmart is a great idea. It's a great vehicle for up-and-coming writers so they can get in front of people to pitch and sell. It teaches them how to get their story down to two minutes, which can be brutal.

"After I sent out four or five copies of my script, I got calls saying, 'We want to move forward,' and I had to make a decision on which one I wanted to go with. That was kind of nice.

"Even Ken called me and said he had a major studio that wanted to do it. But we already had a deal. I basically went with Animal Planet for a couple of reasons: one because I really trusted the producer that I pitched it to, and two, the deal I got was very fair. Better than most people get for a first screenplay.

"Also, they were the first one to say, 'Yes, we believe it. We see it.' I even interviewed other companies but most wanted to change the story, wanted to make it more Disney or more Rambo or wanted to alter the structure. I just didn't feel like that was the right thing to do.

"Now they all want to see what else I have. It's kind of nice. If I was a prolific writer, and wanted to go in that direction, I might be able to get some other stuff made. But since I wrote *Rain*, I've gone into business and I'm doing well.

And finally, Ken's prophesy came true. He said if *Rain* didn't get made, he'd leave the entertainment business. Now, he doesn't have to leave."

GEORGE FERRIS

"Originally, my screenplay, *Styx*, went through Brad Pollock at Skylark. But, as so often happens, he was not involved in the final phase.

"In fact, we were both pretty much on the sidelines by the time the movie was made. I wrote the script back in 1992–1993, and I pitched it to Brad about that time. He actually optioned it for a period of about a year.

"I had already taken it to Gil Wishnick, and she passed on it. I don't recall when, but Brad took it to her again, and what was amazing was that he got her to jump aboard.

"Jon Kramer, president at Promark Entertainment Group, liked the idea of one brother going back to help another brother, plus I kept hearing that Jon wanted this film to be made.

"There was a very long gestation period. It didn't get into Promark's hands until 1995 or 1996. Their option kicked in for an initial period of a year and a half and then a second period of a year and a half. They used every minute of it. I got my final check for it in 2000.

"They filmed it in South Africa the summer of 2000. But the script went through several generations. First, was my original version. Then we took it in and worked with Gil who massaged and changed it. I have to admit, she improved it. I might not have said that a couple of years ago, but the truth is, I think she made it better than it was.

"A lot of the elements are still there, although the final version bears no relationship to the original script. The older brother goes back to rescue a younger brother and gets enmeshed in a life of crime. At least that much is intact. They kept the robbery element, although it's much different than what I had originally written.

"They brought in another writer who rewrote about two-thirds of the script. The last half is completely new. However, there are still some recognizable elements in this version.

"Then the director, a guy named Alex Wright, came in and completely rewrote it. Very little of my draft remained except, strangely enough, many of the character names stayed largely the same. My main character Nelson Reddy became Nelson Reedy. No big deal. Lurie is the same and so is Tipton. DaCosta, a Portuguese spelling, became DeCosta, which is also no big deal.

"The kernel of the script originally was to take the Orpheus legend and try to translate it into modern crime terms. That kind of fell by the wayside, but the title is a hangover from that. I can't imagine what the title has to do with the script now. But 'Styx' is there and *Styx* it shall stay.

"I've seen the trailer, not the film. It looks like an action picture. I don't know how good it is yet. Will I see it when it comes out? Of course!

"I think the cast is very good: Peter Weller, Bryan Brown, and Angus MacFadyen, who played Robert the Bruce in *Braveheart*. These are significant names and it's been my biggest, although it's not 100% my script, my biggest success so far.

"I got the credit. I got the money. Two out of three ain't bad.

"The pitch on *Styx* was very simple because I pushed the brother angle. I guess I'd put it this way."

STYX

Nelson Reddy is a man who runs an auto parts store, but he has a past in crime. His younger brother Mike is a nice guy, but totally feckless and can't get his act together, and because of gambling, is in up to his neck with a loan shark. In order to save Mike from a terrible fate, Nelson must go back into his past in crime to participate in a robbery.

The robbery is to take place in a desert town. A truck filled with rocket fuel is parked in the middle of town and our guys (who are bluffing) threaten to blow it up. But then Nelson realizes that the plan all along is to detonate the truck after the robbery and escape in the ensuing holocaust.

That's when Nelson jumps ship and asks Mike to go with him. Initially Mike won't, but eventually he does. The wrinkle: the local sheriff is one of Nelson's former gang members. When he sees Nelson back in town, he surmises that Nelson's reason for coming to this town is either to commit a robbery, or more likely, to shake him down because of his past.

So, he reacts decisively and violently.

"That's the pitch!

"There's a strong influence of *One-Eyed Jacks* in the film, which was sort of a subsequent influence. I've always liked *One-Eyed Jacks*.

"I'm glad *Styx* was made. People are impressed that my name is on a film with Peter Weller, Bryan Brown and Angus MacFadyen. It's a step up in my career. I'm presently negotiating for another film. Who can say what this will lead to?"

DAVE STAUFFER

"A few years ago, Ken held a private pitch session for Producer Ron Jacobs, who wasn't able to attend the previous Pitchmart. Ron had a multi-picture deal with PM Productions, and he brought several of their executives with him.

"I was the only person in the workshop who researched the kind of films PM made — action-packed thrillers. I rented several of their videos, so I had a good idea of what they were looking for.

"I pitched a couple of ideas in their genre and they responded, indicating that they wanted to hear more. I was invited to their offices to pitch.

"I was going to school part-time and wasn't sure I could attend all the meetings required if I got an assignment, so I called a friend, George Ferris, who I'd gone to USC Film School with. I knew George was a good writer. I suggested we team up. That way at least one of us could make the meetings.

"We ended up going in and getting shot down probably three or four times over the course of a year. Each time we were sure they wouldn't call us back, but for some reason, they did. All the time, we were trying to come up with a concept that would work.

"I wanted to do something different in the low-budget action genre, and I started thinking about a computer school where there were several Russians students. It was in a bad neighborhood. I thought, 'What about a female Charles Bronson? What if there was a woman who used to be a Russian agent and she's over here now, but nobody knows about her past?

"'Her family's over here too. Recent immigrants, maybe they own a little Mom and Pop corner store. Then something bad happens to them; maybe a sister is raped and killed by a gang and the lead, this woman, with all her training, goes after the gang and kicks ass.'

"When I mentioned the idea in the workshop, Ken said he'd written a sitcom pilot for the comedy team Martin & Rossi. In the pilot, one of them marries a Russian woman who quickly adapts to the American way of doing things. Ken suggested the lead be a housewife in the San Fernando Valley. It seemed to click.

"That became the concept. From there, George and I worked out the plot line. It was a pretty straightforward story, where her past catches up to her.

"It piqued interest. Gathered momentum. Finally, it looked like a greenlight. We left Ron's office on a Friday as they were staffing up. They were going to make offers to talent. But by Monday, everything was dead. The funding fell through.

"Cut to two years later. We ran into Ron at an industry function. He had another deal with PM in place and needed an action piece.

"He had just done a picture for PM with Jeff Speakman the year before. He remembered our script. But the old script wouldn't do. PM needed a male lead for the foreign markets. Action pictures usually need male leads to do well.

"We did a rewrite, actually more like another script, but we kept the central concept of a former commando now living in America and no one knows about his past.

"But Jeff had scripts by other writers he liked and we heard he had concerns about playing a Russian, a former Soviet operative. We addressed his concerns in a rewrite with Ron's input and the changes made it a better script.

"In the dead period between our first effort with a female-lead script and what became the film starring Jeff Speakman, we pitched it around a bit. It usually got a good response.

"It's a great feeling knowing you have a pitch that works. It's like going into a poker game with a full house. You may not win with a full house, but you've got a damn good chance.

"It got so I could anticipate the reactions of the development people. I got a sense of what worked, and I further honed the pitch 'til I was pretty sure of the response I was going to get.

"But every once in a while, someone would throw us a curve. They would just not get it or react off the wall. The thing to remember is, it might have nothing to do with you. The executive might have had a fight with his wife or he hates the company he's working for. At that point, remember, it only takes one company to say 'yes.' Treat it like a numbers game.

"But most of the time, if you have a pitch that works, you know it. You get used to hearing the same response at the same time. It's like singing an old standard, where you know the audience is going to cheer or hush at certain points. And then you can relax and enjoy giving your performance.

"I'm a little rusty at it, but here's how the pitch went."

RUNNING RED

I have an action thriller for you called *Running Red*. It starts ten years ago overseas. There's a secret commando raid on a chemical plant that is producing illegal weapons. The twist is these commandos are Russian.

During the mission, one man is killed. He's the younger brother of our hero, who is enraged and shaken by his loss.

Cut to ten years later. He's in the United States, living in the San Fernando Valley. The cold war is over. His past is behind him. He speaks fluent English; everyone thinks he's an American. He's happily married, with a child and a good job. No one knows about his past.

Until he gets a call from his old Russian Commander who is in the States. He's found our hero. He's forcing him back for one final mission: to kill three men.

The first target is the man who killed his brother. The lead has sworn vengeance against him, so he's not reluctant to make that hit. The second target is equally despicable, a drug lord in cahoots with the man who killed his brother. But they won't tell him the third target.

He goes on his mission. At great risk, he accomplishes the first kill and gets vengeance for his brother. He has no problem with the second hit. As far as he's concerned, it's over.

But they want him to make one more hit. An innocent person. He tries to walk away, but they kidnap his family. Now he's caught in a dilemma: Is he going to kill an innocent man or watch his family die? Would you like to read the script?

"That's the pitch.

"When you're actively pitching, you're constantly practicing, getting the words down pat, certain words, particular phrases, etc., 'til it's like a recording. That enables you to relax and put on a performance.

"One day, when I pitched the old script, an executive asked, 'Did you read the trades today?' I said, 'No.' 'Well, there's an article about a famous writer. He just sold a script for four million dollars.' 'What's it about?', I asked. 'It's the same story,' he said. 'You're kidding!' was about all I could say.

"That's the way some people in Hollywood think. They're always comparing story elements and they sometimes make the wildest similarities into a shorthand that typecasts stories. Like saying *The Poseidon Adventure* and *Titanic* are the same since they're both about ships. This was just one of those coincidences.

"Even when the actual stories are close, beginners make the assumption someone's trying to rob their story, to rip them off, when it's really just parallel development. It seems to happen all the time. I just wish I'd gotten the four million."

PHIL OLSON

"In a setting like Ken's Pitchmart, where you have many writers pitching to numerous producers, you may only get three minutes to pitch your script before having to move on to the next producer. If you meet with a producer in their office you will probably get a little more time. If that is the case it's always good to do your homework before meeting with the producer. What films have they produced? What are they working on now? What genre do they do best? Make it a point to see something they've done. In their office, you get a chance to kind of relax, so to speak, and warm up to the people a little.

"I've been in sales for many years, and as Dale Carnegie would say, 'if you want someone to like you, get them to talk about themselves and show sincere interest in what they are saying.' If you like golf and they have a golf trophy in their office, or a movie poster of a film you really liked, or a Starbucks cup on their desk, or you have a friend in common, whatever it is, find an ice-breaker. Something they are interested in.

"*Crappie Talk* is a play I wrote that was produced to critical acclaim in Los Angeles and in Minnesota. It also won a few awards including a National Playwright Competition. I adapted the play into a low-budget screenplay and into a sitcom. Frankly, it's better as a sitcom, but original sitcoms are very difficult to get on the networks, unless you've been a producer on a successful series.

I have pitched *Crappie Talk* to several producers with good success. The success, I think, is in the presentation. Being from a sales background and having acting experience, I tend to get a little theatrical in my presentation. Being enthusiastic and entertaining is important. Especially with comedies.

"Because *Crappie Talk* was a produced play with several rave reviews, I'll typically start the pitch by showing them a flyer from the play with the reviews on it, and mentioning the awards it has won. The *Los Angeles Times* called the play 'a two-hour pilot for a television series, *Cheers* meets *WKRP* meets *Newhart*... and throw in *Fargo* too.' That seems to get their attention and gives the script a kind of credibility.

"Personal history is always good in these pitches. If you can relate it to something that happened in your life, that's good. I grew up in Minnesota in a Scandinavian family and that's part of my pitch.

"My parents are of Norwegian descent. My dad grew up in North Dakota, my mom in Minnesota. My parents were actually related before they were married. No kidding. Not a brother-sister *Deliverance* kind of relationship, but second cousins removed kind of thing. At any rate, it's pretty wacky, and people are amused by that.

"I tend to write stories about where I'm from and I would say I'm probably as qualified as anybody to write about the Scandinavian culture in Minnesota. That's what inspired me to write about the people that I grew up with, which are those people you see in *Crappie Talk*.

"When I begin my pitch, I use a Minnesota accent, and that always seems to be entertaining for people. They like that *Fargo* stuff. So, half of my pitch is based on the delivery and the theatricality of the presentation. *Crappie Talk* is a Minnesota love story with jingles."

CRAPPIE TALK

The setting is Whitefish Bay, Minnesota, up near the Canadian border, and proud home of Ole's Bait Mart, which is just a half mile north of Ole's Deer Petting Farm on route 22, where you can have your picture taken next to the world's oldest moose. And Saturday is 'pronto pup day' for the kiddies. Just on the other side of Ole's Bait Mart you got Ole's Lutheran Hall of Fame where first-time visitors receive a free glass of grape juice in the new herring and wafer bar, which is just down the hall from the Chapel of Good Intentions.

147

"I've had producers say 'stop right there. I want to read it, you don't have to go any further. Based on what you just did, I'll read it."

> One of the locations is: Carl and Linda's Place for Beer where people come from far and near, to drink Hamms and Schlitz and Grain Belt too, and a bowl full of pretzels that you can chew.

"That's one of the jingles, of course."

> In the bar is a tiny radio station, K-O-L-D radio Whitefish Bay. It's about the size of a large closet. The main guy, Lars Knudsen, is the host of a radio show called *Crappie Talk*. A Crappie is a fish. Lars devotes his entire show to talking about ice fishing for crappies. Kind of a narrow subject.

> Lars has no listeners. Not one, seriously, nada, none. So he loses his only advertiser, Ole's Bait Mart. This makes Lars mad. Martha Bjorklund is Lars' love interest. She's the host of a radio show called *Book Beat*. Martha has all the advertisers. She's got all the listeners too, and this really makes Lars mad. You see, Lars has issues: Martha beat Lars in the 50-yard Snow Shoe Sprint in the fifth grade and Lars never got over it. Issues.

> Enter Sal Carducci and Donna DeCasola, two fish out of water, Brooklyn Italians. Donna divorced Sal because he was a scumbag, and ran away to the farthest corner of the world to get away from him, Whitefish Bay. Well, Sal followed Donna to Whitefish Bay and in the process of trying to win back her love, he buys the radio station, promotes Martha to general manager and fires Lars.

Now this really makes Lars mad. I mean, he needs his dignity, he needs his job. But most important, he needs Martha.

"That's basically the pitch. I'll vary it depending on who my audience is and what kind of a feedback I'm getting from the executives. Sometimes they'll stop and ask me questions right then and there, so I'll answer the questions.

"I've had good success with producers requesting to read *Crappie Talk* based on my pitch. Its success as a play helps but producers seem to be entertained by the pitch and that's what gets them to want to read it. *Crappie Talk* has been optioned by a few production companies for both a film and a television series. I've had interest from very high levels. Some day it will be made. But not right now.

"*Crappie Talk* is a little too rural for television at this time. Hollywood goes in cycles. Right now, it's all about *Friends*. Show us something with young good-looking people in an apartment in the city. However, with the advent of a few recent quirky *Northern Exposure* type series like *Ed* set in Stuckyville, Ohio, we will soon dust off *Crappie Talk* and start to pitch it again. The trend seems to be coming back. Never give up. Sooner or later, you'll wear them down.

"Writing plays and getting them produced is a great way to learn how to write. If you go through the stage reading process that I went through, plus the support of Ken's Workshop, it's a great way to go. Having staged readings, where actors are cast in the various roles, allows you to hear your lines being read. It also allows you to hear feedback on your work from the audience and make changes based on the feedback.

"When you see your play performed a number of times in front of a live audience and watch their reactions, you can see what works and what doesn't. I continued to fine-tune the play during its run. Although it's not common, several plays have been made into movies, *Glengarry Glen Ross*, *American Buffalo*, *Driving Miss Daisy*, and *A Few Good Men*, to mention a few.

"You can make a play into a very inexpensive movie. For the most part, plays are not big blockbusters, but if they're done well, they can make money.

"My experience with *Crappie Talk* was so good, I wrote another play, *A Nice Family Gathering*, which was also produced to rave reviews as well as winning a National Playwright Award. Plays are nice because it's not nearly as hard to get them produced as a film. Also, there is no better thrill than to see a live audience respond to your work."

The Group Repertory Theatre *presents*

The National Award-Winning Comedy

CRÄPPIE TALK

Written by Phil Olson

Directed By Mareli Mitchel & Stephen R. Hudis

$2.00 off regular admission with this flyer

HELD OVER !!!! By Popular Demand

"Combine superb comic writing with solid direction and a smart cast with great timing, and you're headed for a comedy hit."
- *LA Weekly*
Pick of the Week

"...hilarious...side-splitting pace... A real audience pleaser, this comedy is totally silly, entertaining and refreshingly unique."
- *Tolucan*

"A heart-warming tale in cold Minnesota where you'll find love, laughter and a wonderful time."
- *Irish News*

This one really reels in the laughs."
- *Arthur Cantor*
Tony-Award Winning Broadway Producer

...Olson has actually come up with a two act pilot for a TV series. In high conceptese, it's *Cheers*, meets *WKRP in Cincinnati*, meets *Newhart* ... and throw in *Fargo*, too..."
- *LA TIMES*

"Set in the American Heartland of Whitefish Bay, it is the plain spoken Minnesotan Story of Lars Knudsen's need to find love..."
- *American Eagle News*

"... a pleasant romantic comedy...very entertaining."
- *Gardena Valley News*

Featuring

Bethany Carpenter
Vince Cefalu
Jennifer Cohen
Robert DiTillio
Doug Engalla

Cynthia Fancher
Jack Goodman
Therese Lentz
Phil Olson
Jill Piwowar

Produced for the GRT by Art Shulman

FRI & SAT at 8:00
SUN at 3:00

Admission
$15.00

Reservations: 818 . 769 - PLAY
Group Sales: Dom Salinaro 818 . 785-7717

On Burbank, 1 Block East of Vineland

10900 Burbank Boulevard
North Hollywood CA 91601

Coming up next at The GRT: *Between Two Thieves* by Warner LeRoy and *Two Grandmas From Brooklyn*

MAKING THIEVES OF US ALL
The Internet: Friend or Foe?

Overheard at the Workshop:

"So I start my pitch. 'The story is about three men....' The producer cuts me off and finishes my sentence, '...who escape from prison.' I'm a little stung, but we're supposed to be quick on our feet. 'Right,' I say, then throw in, 'At night they hide in a barn and...' He interrupts again, '...and find an abandoned baby in a hayloft.' 'Right,' I mumble, plowing on, "The next morning, baby in hand, they leave the barn....' He cuts me off again, '...only to find the sheriff and twenty deputies surrounding the barn, rifles poised.' Now he's really excited and cries out, 'What happens next?' To which I exclaim, 'How the hell do I know? You put them in that mess, you get 'em out!'"

Now, I want to tell you about a form of pitching I don't approve of.

There are numerous sites on the Internet that invite writers to pitch their screenplays for little or no money. They claim that your pitch will reach hundreds of producers and studio executives simultaneously. And if there is interest in your pitch, you will be contacted by the dot.com company and put in touch with the interested party.

Sounds great! Except for one thing.

You have no control over who reads your material. If they steal your story, how can you prove they got the idea off the Internet?

The only way you can protect your story — beyond registering it with the Library of Congress or the Writers Guild — is to have a paper trail from you to the guilty party.

Do not — I repeat — do not put your stories — either pitches or screenplays — on the Internet. The idea sounds great — terrific exposure — but you're just as apt to get ripped off as you are to make a legitimate deal.

(Note: A possible exception might be something like the joint Miramax, Damon/Affleck, HBO Project Greenlight. These are all reputable people and organizations, but you are still turning over your screenplay to the great unknown, and it is a very new approach to contests, so "contributor beware.")

In any event, look what's happening to studio-bought screenplays. For decades, studios *NEVER* allowed anyone who wasn't directly involved with the production to see a script. Screenplays were top secret, guarded against the prying eyes of outsiders. Stories were hush-hush until the trailers came out, when it would be too late for anyone to steal the idea.

Then along came the Internet and everything changed. Today, first-draft screenplays, pre-release reviews, and yes, even pitches, are splashed across a plethora of Internet sites. What used to be private is now open to anyone and everyone.

While studio executives, independent producers and filmmakers are taking extreme measures to assure security, somehow, some way, there are leaks allowing Internet sites to have a field day at the writers' expense.

One agent told me this story. His writer-client put his pitch on the Internet. Since each pitch is only given a number, no one knew who the writer was, nor his agent. The agent said he got a phone call from a friend who wanted to know if the agent saw this particular pitch.

The agent, having known the story, said he had. His friend then told him that he should find out who the writer is and sign him. The friend said the buzz all over town was that the story was a winner and that three studios had already hired writers to write a screenplay *based on this agent's client's pitch on the Internet*!

So don't blindly put out information on your script. You lose control. If your idea is unique, commercial, or cinematic, it's just too tempting for someone to snatch it away from you.

You have been warned!

IN CONCLUSION
Telling It Like It Is.

Overheard at the Workshop:

"So I said to my husband, 'I'm gonna pitch the hell out of this baby. They're gonna buy it for three mil; we'll move to a bigger house; get in with a fast crowd; start taking drugs; become addicts; go to Betty Ford; then, we'll end up getting divorced and going our separate ways.' I thought for a second, 'Maybe I won't pitch it.'"

"Mr. Rotcop, please come this way." We pass secretary after secretary after secretary and I start to think that all these secretaries are prisoners on death row. The secretary I'm following is the warden and I am being led to an execution. In truth, I'm about to meet the creative head of a production company and pitch my screenplay. I hope he doesn't press a button that will send an electrical bolt through my body and kill me and my story forever.

On the way down this long hallway past all these secretaries, I begin to doubt myself.

How dare I call myself a writer? How dare I try to compete with the Rod Serlings and the David E. Kellys and the Steven J. Cannells and the Arthur Millers and the Ernest Hemingways? How dare I think that what I have to say is as important as what they said, or that I could say it as eloquently? How dare I compete with them?

But as I continue past all these secretaries, I begin to think of all the hours I put in creating this story. All the hours I spent with those characters who sat on my shoulder, who burned in my brain, who were there with me day and night, helping me to get through this script, helping to plot the story, helping me create the arcs of each of their lives. I begin to say to myself, damn it, I can do this. I have something to say. Maybe I'm not Serling or Kelly or Miller or Hemingway, but damn it, I have a script that I'm proud of. And I'm going to do the best I can to sell it. I owe it to my characters!

I enter the office of the executioner, oops, the producer. We are introduced and we chit-chat for a bit. He then says to me, "What have you got?"

So I start with an anecdote that gets him in a good mood. I tell him how I came up with my story. I tell him the genre and then I begin.

"My story is about..."

He's about to hear The Perfect Pitch. The same kind you're going to deliver at your next pitch meeting. Go get 'em, tiger!

THE END

KEN ROTCOP'S
PROFESSIONAL WRITERS WORKSHOP

Ken Rotcop works with would-be and professional writers one-on-one — on their screenplays, manuscripts, or plays — to help writers sell their work.

Writers from all over the country as well as Canada and the Philippines currently work long-distance with Rotcop using the phone, e-mail, and postal services to communicate.

Once Rotcop deems a script is ready for the market, he will get the writer a literary agent or manager for representation.

The writer will be invited to the twice-a-year Pitchmarts, a forum for pitching scripts to over twenty executives and producers from networks, production companies, and studios. Many scripts have been optioned because of the Pitchmart.™

Another feature of the workshop is the annual showcase in which professional actors do readings of scenes from students' works. Invited guests include executives, agents, and producers. Again, numerous deals have resulted from these showcases.

For further information contact Ken Rotcop directly:

Phone: (818) 883-0554
E-mail: Pitchmart@Juno.com
Mail: Ken Rotcop
4434 Canoga Avenue
Woodland Hills, CA 91364

Script Magic
Subconscious Techniques to Conquer Writer's Block

Marisa D'Vari

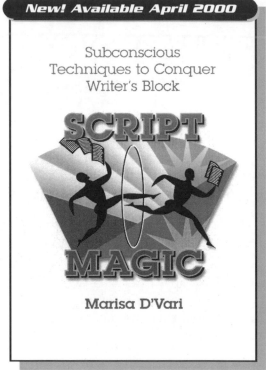

Script Magic answers the prayers of every screenwriter who's ever spent time staring down a blank page. Pursuing the dream of landing that big script sale can be stressful, and that stress and pressure can be counter-productive to the writing process. *Script Magic* is a powerful antidote to writer's block that both professional and aspiring creative writers can benefit from, based on a deceptively simple principle: If you're not having fun writing it, your script probably isn't going to be any fun to read, either. And if it's not fun to read, how is it ever going to be sold and made into a movie that people will want to spend their money to see?

Using easy and fun techniques designed to circumvent the practical, critical conscious mind and tap into the rich creative resources of the subconscious mind, readers will learn how to revitalize their writing and improve their productivity. Create engaging characters, dialogue that jumps off the page and screenplays that sell!

MARISA D'VARI has 20 years of hands-on experience working in Hollywood as a studio story analyst, consultant and executive. She currently produces and hosts her own nationally syndicated cable TV show, "Scene Here," and conducts seminars on screenwriting all over the country. Visit her Web site at **www.scriptmagic.com**.

Doubleday Stage & Screen Selection

$18.95, ISBN 0-941188-74-4
250 pages, 6 x 9
Order # 47RLS

The Writer's Journey

—2nd Edition

Mythic Structure for Writers

Christopher Vogler

1st Edition - Over 100,000 Sold!

See why this book has become an international best seller, and a true classic. First published in 1992, *The Writer's Journey* explores the powerful relationship between mythology and storytelling in a clear, concise style that's made it required reading for movie executives, screenwriters, scholars, and lovers of pop culture all over the world.

Writers of both fiction and non-fiction will discover a set of useful myth-inspired storytelling paradigms (i.e. *The Hero's Journey*) and step-by-step guidelines to plot and character development. Based on the work of Joseph Campbell, *The Writer's Journey* is a must for writers of all kinds interested in further developing their craft.

The updated and revised 2nd edition provides new insights and observations from Vogler's ongoing work on mythology's influence on stories, movies, and man himself.

> *"This is a book about the stories we write, and perhaps more importantly, the stories we live. It is the most influential work I have yet encountered on the art, nature, and the very purpose of storytelling."*
> **Bruce Joel Rubin**, Screenwriter, *Ghost, Jacob's Ladder*

Book of the Month Club Selection • Writer's Digest Book Club Selection • Movie Entertainment Book Club Selection • Doubleday Stage and Screen Selection

CHRIS VOGLER has been a top Hollywood story consultant and development executive for over 15 years. He has worked on such top grossing feature films as *The Thin Red Line*, *Fight Club*, *The Lion King*, and *Beauty and the Beast*. His international workshops have taken him to Germany, Italy, United Kingdom and Spain, and his literary consulting service Storytech provides in-depth evaluations for professional writers. To learn more, visit his Web site at **www.thewritersjourney.com**.

$22.95, ISBN 0-941188-70-1
300 pages, 6 x 9
Order # 98RLS

Myth & the Movies

Discovering the Mythic Structure of 50 Unforgettable Films

Stuart Voytilla

Foreword by **CHRISTOPHER VOGLER**, author of "The Writer's Journey"

With this collection of essays exploring the mythic structure of 50 well-loved U.S. and foreign films, Voytilla has created a fun and fascinating book for film fans, screenwriters, and anyone with a love of storytelling and pop culture.

An informal companion piece to the best-selling *The Writer's Journey* by Christopher Vogler, *Myth and the Movies* applies the mythic structure Vogler developed to films as diverse as "Die Hard," "Singin' in the Rain" and "Boyz N the Hood." This comprehensive book offers a greater understanding of why some films continue to touch and connect with audiences generation after generation.

Movies discussed include *Annie Hall, Beauty and the Beast, Chinatown, Citizen Kane, E.T., The Fugitive, The Godfather, The Graduate, La Strada, The Piano, Pulp Fiction, Notorious, Raiders of the Lost Ark, The Searchers, The Silence of the Lambs, T2–Judgment Day, Sleepless in Seattle, Star Wars, Unforgiven,* and many more.

STUART VOYTILLA is a writer, script consultant, and teacher of acting and screenwriting. He has evaluated hundreds of scripts for LA -based talent agencies. His latest screenplay, *The Golem*, is being produced by Baltimore-based Princess Pictures.

Movie Entertainment Book Club Selection

$26.95, ISBN 0-941188-66-3
300 pages, 7 x 10, illustrations throughout
Order # 39RLS

Stealing Fire From the Gods

A Dynamic New Story Model for Writers and Filmmakers

James Bonnet

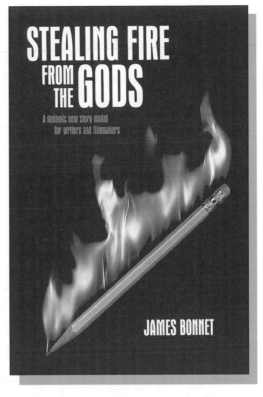

Great stories affect us so much because they teach us about life, and about ourselves. In the tradition of Carl Jung, Joseph Campbell and Christopher Vogler, James Bonnet explores the connection between mythology and personal growth—and the implications that connection has for storytellers in particular.

Unlike films, novels, and other forms of modern storytelling we're accustomed to today, the great myths, legends and fairy tales passed down through the ages were not created by individual authors. They evolved from ancient oral traditions, fueled by forces within the creative unconscious that are still accessible to us today. *Stealing Fire From the Gods* investigates those forces and teaches writers how to use the same elements that make those traditional tales so enduring to make your own stories more powerful, memorable and emotionally resonant. Author James Bonnet takes you on a journey through the creative process of storytelling, uncovering not only what makes a story great but also how the creative process can reconnect us to our lost or forgotten inner selves.

JAMES BONNET, founder of Astoria Filmwrights, is a successful Hollywood screen and television writer. He has acted in or written more than forty television shows and features including *Kojak*, *Barney Miller* and the cult classics *The Blob* and *The Cross and The Switchblade*. Visit his Web site at **www.storymaking.com**.

Movie Entertainment Book Club Selection

$26.95, ISBN: 0-941188-65-5
300 pages, 6 x 9
Order # 38RLS

Writing the Second Act

Building Conflict and Tension in Your Film Script

Michael Halperin, Ph.D.

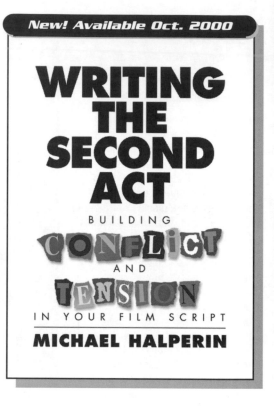

New! Available Oct. 2000

WRITING THE SECOND ACT

BUILDING CONFLICT AND TENSION

IN YOUR FILM SCRIPT

MICHAEL HALPERIN

Every screenplay needs an attention-grabbing beginning and a satisfying ending, but those elements are nothing without a strong, well-crafted middle. The second act is where most of the action is: where your characters grow, change, and overcome the obstacles that will bring them to the resolution at the end of the story. Naturally, it's also the hardest act to write, and where most screenplays tend to lose momentum and focus. Author Halperin helps you slay the dragon with *Writing the Second Act*, designed especially for helping screenwriters through that crucial 60-page stretch. Structural elements and plot devices are discussed in detail, as well as how to keep the action moving and the characters evolving while keeping the audience completely absorbed in and entertained by your story.

MICHAEL HALPERIN is a professional writer whose numerous credits include TV shows (*Star Trek: The Next Generation*, *Quincy*), nonfiction books (*Writing Great Characters*), and interactive media programs (*Voyeur*). He has also worked extensively as a consultant in the television industry, including Executive Story Consultant for 20th Century Fox Television and Creative Consultant on the animated series *Masters of the Universe*. He currently teaches screenwriting at Loyola Marymount University in Los Angeles and is in the process of developing a business-to-business Web site for the entertainment industry.

$19.95, ISBN 0-941188-29-9
240 Pages, 6 x 9
Order # 49RLS

Freelance Writing for Hollywood

How to Pitch, Write and Sell Your Work

Scott Essman

New! Available June 2000

Do you read movie reviews or feature stories on your favorite artists and think to yourself, "I could do that?" Ever wondered how you can turn your love of movies and pop culture into money in your pocket? Consider the possibilities of the vast and varied field of entertainment writing.

Freelance Writing for Hollywood is your guide to this wide-ranging, exciting field. Whether you're an experienced journalist or a novice looking to break in, this book provides valuable tips and sound advice on everything from constructing a well-written feature to targeting the publications and markets best for you. Topics range from fundamentals such as defining goals, choosing subject matter and selecting a medium, to advanced subjects such as networking, cold-calling, pitching your idea and self-publishing. Whatever your experience level, this book will help you find your niche in the field of entertainment writing and give you the tools you need to be successful in it.

SCOTT ESSMAN is a seasoned freelance writer and independent theater producer. His articles have appeared in *The Los Angeles Times*, *Cinefex*, *MovieMaker* and *L'Ecran Fantastique*, among other publications.

$19.95, ISBN 0-941188-27-2
280 pages, 6 x 9
Order # 48RLS

Screenwriting 101
The Essential Craft of Feature Film Writing

Neill D. Hicks

Hicks, a successful screenwriter whose credits include *Rumble in the Bronx* and *First Strike*, brings the clarity and practical instruction familiar to his UCLA students to screenwriters everywhere. In his refreshingly straightforward style, Hicks tells the beginning screenwriter how the mechanics of Hollywood storytelling work, and how to use those elements to create a script with blockbuster potential without falling into cliches. Also discussed are the practicalities of the business—securing an agent, pitching your script, protecting your work, and other topics essential to building a career in screenwriting.

"Neill Hicks makes complex writing concepts easy to grasp, in a way that only a master teacher could. And he does so while keeping his book one hell of a fun read."
Eric Edson, Screenwriter and Executive Director of the Hollywood Symposium

NEILL HICKS is a professional screenwriter and a senior instructor at the UCLA Extension Writer's Program, where he has been honored with the Outstanding Instructor Award. He has also taught graduate courses on screenwriting at the University of Denver, presented a seminar on Selling to Hollywood at the Denver International Film Festival, and conducts screenwriting workshops throughout the United States, Canada, and Europe. Visit his Web site at **www.screenwriting101.net**.

Movie Entertainment Book Club Selection
Doubleday Stage and Screen Selection

$16.95, ISBN 0-941188-72-8
220 pages, 6 x 9
Order # 41RLS

Fade In: The Screenwriting Process
—2nd Edition

Bob Berman

A classic used by professionals and
universities around the world since the
first edition debuted in 1988, *Fade In*
is a concise, step-by-step road map for
developing a story concept into a finished screenplay. In addition to cover-
ing the basics of screenwriting—everything from structure and character
development to terminology, form and
writing revisions, Berman shares his
experiences as a screenwriter who got
his start relatively late in life. Readers
can glean valuable tips and insights on
the realities of breaking into the professional screenwriting "biz" and how
the whole system works, from getting
your script read to getting an agent to
making deals.

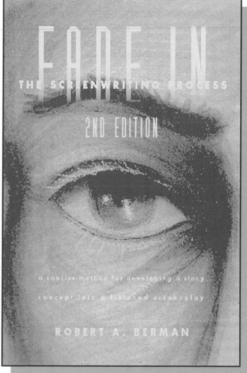

Also included is the author's original
script, *Dead Man's Dance*, complete
with an agent's critique of this screenplay.

BOB BERMAN is a screenwriter and a professional nonfiction writer. He currently lives
in Westchester County, New York where he has begun work on a new screenplay and
conducts private script consultations.

$24.95, ISBN 0-941188-58-2
350 pages, 6 x 8-1/4
Order # 30RLS

MICHAEL WIESE PRODUCTIONS

11288 Ventura Blvd., Suite 821
Studio City, CA 91604
1-818-379-8799
kenlee@earthlink.net
www.mwp.com

Write or Fax
for a
free catalog.

Please send me the following books:

Title   Order Number (#RLS___)   Amount

_____ _____

_____ _____

_____ _____

_____ _____

                    SHIPPING   _____

        California Tax (8.25%)   _____

            TOTAL ENCLOSED _____

Please make check or money order payable to
Michael Wiese Productions

(Check one) ___ Master Card ___Visa ___Amex

Credit Card Number_____

Expiration Date_____

Cardholder's Name_____

Cardholder's Signature_____

SHIP TO:

Name_____

Address_____

City_____State_____Zip_____